JACK GIBSON'S FUR COAT

Gatora

Glen Humphries

JACK GIBSON'S FUR COAT

RUGBY LEAGUE ODDITIES AND ARTEFACTS

GELDING STREET PRESS

For mum and dad, even though she doesn't like rugby league and he prefers union.

A Gelding Street Press book
An Imprint of Rockpool Publishing, Pty Ltd.

PO Box 252,
Summer Hill
NSW 2130, Australia

www.geldingstreetpress.com
Follow us! geldingstreet_press

Published in 2023 by Gelding Street Press

ISBN: 9780645207132

Design and typesetting by Daniel Poole, Rockpool Publishing
Edited by Heather Millar
Acquisition editor: Luke West, Rockpool Publishing

A catalogue record for this book is available from the National Library of Australia

Printed and bound in China
10 9 8 7 6 5 4 3 2 1

CONTENTS

‘THAT BLOODY COAT . . . IT WEIGHED A TONNE. I COULD BARELY PICK IT UP.’

WHATEVER HAPPENED TO THAT LEGENDARY COAT IS A MYSTERY.

INTRODUCTION

If you're of a certain age, you remember Jack Gibson's fur coat. It was a brown coat made of kangaroo pelts that he sported for the 1983 grand final. He loved that coat, even though the sheer weight of the thing aggravated a back complaint; that was why he spent much of the game watching his Eels play Manly from the stands, his arms and chin resting on the railing in front of him. His back ached less that way.

But he wasn't going to take it off. And so there are photos of him on the field after the game, celebrating Parramatta's 18-6 win over the minor premiers – a threepeat. There he is with his arm around Peter Sterling, the halfback with a Sea Eagles jersey tied across his shoulders. There's Jack and the coat again, in between Eric Grothe and Stan Jurd – both wearing Manly jerseys (something which has to be explained every time some outlet runs that image). He's also there with a hand on the Winfield Cup; he's grasping Norm Provan by the thigh while Eels boss Denis Fitzgerald on the other side holds Arthur Summons around the waist. And he's there next to newly elected Prime Minister Bob Hawke, the latter hoping for some of the Gibson magic to rub off on him. That fur coat is there in every photo.

Whatever happened to that legendary coat is a mystery. Gibson's wife Judy told his biographer Andrew Webster that it was lost forever. 'That bloody coat,' Judy told him. 'It weighed a tonne. I could barely pick it up. Jack lost it in transit when we were going through LAX [Los Angeles International Airport] in the 1980s. He was very upset – but I couldn't have been happier.'

But 2000 premiership winner Harvey Howard says different. In 2021 Howard told *The Daily Telegraph* Gibson gave it to him. Howard, who was on the bench for Brisbane's 14-6 grand final win over the Roosters, had played most of his six seasons with Wests but his first year in the top grade was at Easts, where he became friends with Gibson.

After the 2000 grand final, the England-born forward was heading home to play in the Super League.

'So I called around to see Jack, say my goodbyes,' Howard remembered. 'But as I'm leaving he says "I've got something for you, something to keep you warm in the UK".'

'Then he brought out the coat. I said "Oh, Jack. I can't take that". But he said "It'll keep you warm".' And so he took it, but not before getting Gibson to autograph it on the inside.

But Howard said the coat never made it to the UK. Along with some other valuables, he had placed it inside a new Mitsubishi Pajero that he was shipping over to the UK. The car was stolen from the shipping container before it made it off the docks in Sydney. A few weeks later, police spotted the car and gave chase, causing the thief to crash. Upon arrest, the thief said he had chucked away the coat that was in the car.

Still, Howard wasn't so sure, which is why he will occasionally cast an eye over the racks at op shops and antique stores just in case it turns up.

Rugby league is full of stories like Gibson's coat. Stories that live on the margins, have fallen through the cracks or simply gone unnoticed. This book captures a number of those tales. Some of them mark significant moments, such as the start of a women's rugby league competition in 1921, to early moves to create an entirely new code of football by merging league and Australian rules.

There are also the unusual tales, like the time several Canterbury-Bankstown players took to the field drunk in 1947, the very same year the NSW representative team was kicked out of a Queensland hotel after trashing a few rooms.

There are also some on-field moments, such as coaches making a mess of replacement rules and costing their team a finals spot, claims Newtown threw the 1944 premiership decider and the first night football match, which occurred a lot earlier than you might expect.

So relax and enjoy some of the stories that contribute to the rich and vivid tapestry of rugby league.

SOUTHS . . . WERE DECLARED THE 1909 SEASON'S PREMIERS IN WHAT ONE PAPER DECLARED 'A FIASCO'.

1

A ONE-SIDED PREMIERSHIP DECIDER

The 1909 decider is unusual in that it was played by only one team. Sure, two teams were supposed to show up but one decided to boycott the fixture. The team that showed up – South Sydney – still had to go through the charade of playing before they could be declared winners.

So, on Saturday, 18 September, Souths kicked off against their absent opponent Balmain, picked up the ball, scored a try and were declared the 1909 season's premiers in what one paper declared 'a fiasco'. It was Souths' second straight premiership, having won the inaugural competition the previous year.

To make up for the absence of the final, a rough team of players from other clubs who happened to be there was patched together and they played Souths – and lost 18-10.

The controversy around the match started earlier in the week and stemmed from a risky idea of the league. They had decided to stage three matches between the Kangaroos and the Wallabies.

Risky because it wouldn't be a good look for the new code if the rugby union representatives beat them at their own game. And that's what happened – the Wallabies beat the Kangaroos in the best-of-three series 2-1.

But, fortunately for the fledgling New South Wales Rugby League (NSWRL) the people running rugby union were idiots. They chose to ban all the Wallaby players who took the substantial cash on offer to play in the series. In one fell swoop, the union officials kicked out its best players, sending them into the hands of league. It was a move that strengthened the newcomer in league and damaged union's fortunes for decades to come.

The Kangaroos apparently couldn't hack losing the series. So on Saturday, 12 September, just after the Kangaroos had lost the final match, they called on the league to organise one more game. There was just one issue with that: the final was scheduled for the following weekend. Well, it should have been a problem for the league, but it wasn't.

They decided to take the biggest game of their season and schedule it as a curtain-raiser to the fourth Wallabies-Kangaroos match on 18 September. A large part of the league's motivation was money – it was out of pocket and saw one more game as a chance to recoup their losses.

Obviously making the final a warm-up game for the Wallabies-Kangaroos didn't sit well with some in league circles, partially because the finals series had already been interrupted for several weeks to allow the three-match series to take place. Balmain and Souths had played the matches that qualified them for the final a month earlier on 14 August.

Balmain were particularly incensed, and at a club meeting it was decided not to place a team on the field on the Saturday. 'It being the final match to decide the premiership of league football in NSW for season 1909,' club secretary A Walker wrote in a public letter, 'the action of the NSW league in playing it as an early match to the Wallabies versus Kangaroos is an insult to the teams concerned.' But the league didn't seem to care – the final would stay as scheduled. There was an understanding from Balmain that Souths would also boycott the fixture. But that didn't come to pass, though the Balmain players were shocked to discover Souths all kitted up and taking the field in what was – at best – a dubious move.

Three days after the match, the league accepted the referee's report – which must have been very brief – and therefore South Sydney were declared premiers. It seemed to be a sneaky move with a Balmain delegation waiting outside to call on the league to reschedule the final for the following weekend.

The issue for Balmain was about more than just the insult of playing their match as a warm-up fixture. It was also highly likely the league's actions had breached its own constitution. During league matches, a portion of the gate takings were to be used to pay for ground fees and other related expenses – as per the constitution.

As far as Balmain was concerned, there was a league match scheduled so therefore the league rules should apply. However, the entirety of the takings from that fourth game went into the promoter's pocket, leaving the league in deficit. There was also the unpleasant issue that the match had been promoted as a fundraiser for the South Sydney Hospital and yet it seemed to have received no money either.

At a public meeting Balmain citizens supported the actions of their local team and passed some strident motions against the league. One contended that the proceeds of the match 'were paid away illegally and unconstitutionally'. A second 'condemns the actions of the league committee first in allowing the control of the game to be taken out of the hands of the governing body and secondly in allotting the promoters of the Wallabies v Kangaroos matches to collect and take away the whole of the proceeds without charging the usual fee for the use of our ground and deducting of all advertising, jerseys and other expenses.'

The meeting also chose to start a fund to collect money for a potential legal challenge. While funds were being raised, someone took the curious decision of writing to the Newcastle league seeking support for Balmain's cause. That didn't go well for the Sydney club; the northern league voted not to help them in any way, shape or form. Even worse, the committee stated that 'the Balmain club acted in anything but a sportsmanlike manner in connection with the league final. They are also of the opinion that the league committee were lacking in their duty in not disqualifying the Balmain club for refusing to play when ordered.'

That blow notwithstanding, by November there was enough money in the kitty to investigate taking the league to the Equity Court. And there the matter seems to have ended – there are no further mentions of the dispute in newspaper reports. And, in the unlikely event they did take the matter to court, it's obvious they didn't win because league records still show South Sydney as 1909 premiers – however dubious their win may have been.

2

LEAGUE RULES

In the early years of rugby league, some in charge had so little faith in the worth of the sport that they tried to combine it with Australian rules to make a national sport. And, leaving aside the strong opposition to any such move, they tried to do it three times.

Rugby league had barely come into existence when the first effort was made to merge the two codes. In 1908 no lesser light than Dally Messenger told JJ Giltinan – one of the founders of league – that Aussie rules had much to offer. Messenger felt a game that contained the best features of rugby league and Australian rules 'would be the most wonderful thing in the world of sport.'

That year, while the very first season of rugby league was underway Giltinan headed south to Victoria to float the possibility of amalgamating the games to create what was tagged 'Universal Football'. So it's a little odd that the National Rugby League (NRL) minor premiers are presented with a shield that bears his name, given he tried to kill off the game of rugby league in its earliest years. In July Giltinan said his proposal had been accepted by the Victorian league, who passed it onto the national council.

'Both games will benefit but the Australian rules game must be brought into line with the Northern Union game, though of course the latter must also give away something,' Giltinan said. 'There is not such a vast difference between the two [sports].'

Giltinan's proposal called for 13 players a side, with the aim of the game to kick the ball between the rugby league–style posts – the behind posts were to be eliminated. A crossbar featured between the posts because some in Australian football circles had a problem with goals that rolled in across the ground.

The Sydney Morning Herald immediately spotted what would become a problem for all efforts to create some sort of Universal Football – the off-side rule. In league, players must stay behind the ball to take part in play, while in Aussie rules they can take possession from anywhere on the field.

'The rock the movement is likely to split upon from an Australian [rules] standpoint is the suggestion to introduce off-side,' the *Herald* reported. 'If there is one thing the Victorians have no time for it is that.'

However, it seemed that ambition was the sticking point; the Victorians wanted a code that would only be played in Australia while Giltinan (much like the Super League proponents of the 1990s) overreached and saw the sport being played worldwide. Giltinan didn't stop there either; at a conference held to discuss the universal football concept, he also pledged that league would kill off rugby union in a matter of a few years. It's a curious thing for him to say at a conference that was in effect killing off league and inventing rules for a new game.

The universal football concept returned six years later, in 1914, the year the Great Britain Lions toured Australia and the Australian rules football interstate carnival (held in NSW for the first time) took place.

Charles Brownlow (yes, the guy whose name is on the medal) got things up and running after what he perceived as the underwhelming response to the NSW interstate carnival. A total of 50,000 spectators watched the 14 games – around 3500 per match. He compared that to the 38,000-plus crowds drawn to watch the Lions play Australia. He figured, somewhat naively, that a combined code would therefore draw big crowds in both Victoria and NSW.

Conferences between officials of both codes were held late in 1914, even though there appeared to be little appetite for a merger among fans of either sport. 'The proposed amalgamation, one is afraid, is not taken seriously by anybody outside the immediate officials concerned,' the *Melbourne Leader* reported. 'We may be quite sure that the rugby league people will never sacrifice their present important international standing to evolve a new game, the effect of which would be to abandon forever those interests.' As for Melbourne, the paper stated 'there are too many people devoted to the Australian game to allow its being supplanted by a new code, half rugby, half their own.'

The conference delegates went ahead and devised some rules for this new code. Rather than 13, this time there would be 15 players per side, on a field not more than 160 yards (146 metres) long by 100 yards (91 metres) wide, which would make it both longer and wider than a league field.

The object of the game was to score a try or kick the ball over the crossbar between the posts. The tryscorer would also be the player who attempted the conversion. Scrums – which were the source of complaint even then, with one Sydney reporter noting 'in the majority of instances [they] bordered on farcical' – were to be eliminated and matches would be restarted by an umpire bouncing the ball rather than a team kicking off.

Still, the off-side rule was a point of contention, with Victorian officials rightly concerned that including one would eliminate their game's high points, like spectacular marks. One NSW delegate suggested a compromise unlikely to work: that the off-side rule would only be enforced within the teams' quarters and the centre space be a free area.

Horrie Miller, who was part of the conference, said the league committee that attended was in favour of the amalgamation but wouldn't take things any further until the Australian rules authorities showed their hand. If they were also in favour, there was the likelihood of exhibition matches played in 1915 with a more serious competition in 1916.

Victorian clubs like Melbourne, St Kilda, Geelong, Essendon and Collingwood had ticked off on the rule changes, while Carlton gave the new game cautious approval. However, some floated the idea of a new Australian rules competition starting in competition to universal football. At the time, the Victorian code didn't own the grounds they played on; the owners were cricket clubs who effectively rented out their facilities in winter. *The Sunday Times* put forward the suggestion that five AFL clubs could say no to universal football and start their own league, which the locals would likely prefer to the new code.

The agreed-upon rule changes were put to the state Australian rules bodies, some of which opted to make no decision on the new game – which is a clear suggestion of their lack of enthusiasm. Also, with World War I and a drought affecting the country, officials behind the universal football push decided it might not be the best time to invest heavily in developing a new code and setting up exhibition matches. And there the idea of a merger petered out.

These two attempts should have marked the end of the universal football quest. If a merger was ever going to happen it was when rugby league was new and hadn't gained a strong foothold in NSW and Queensland. But NSWRL secretary Horrie Miller couldn't let his bad idea go. While he was in Melbourne to send off the departing Australian team on its tour of England in 1933, he floated the idea to his opposite number at the Victorian Football League (VFL), Con Hickey.

And so some officials had more conferences about universal football and again looked at the rules, which were largely the same as had been nutted out in 1914. There were a few updates: the need for a running player to bounce the ball was removed, and Australian rules–style goal squares were added in front of the goal posts at each end of the field.

These conferences went ahead despite a number of NSWRL delegates being opposed to the new code. Most strident was president Harry Flegg, who refused to attend the August conference and blasted universal football supporters as traitors to rugby league. 'In my opinion this conference is nothing but a direct move against rugby league,' he said. 'There's nothing wrong with our game. We have always made any alterations necessary for the improvement of the game.

'It is impossible to combine our game with another. There is absolutely nothing in common. Even if we did combine and had 90 per cent of our rules and only 10 per cent of theirs it would still not be rugby league.'

Rather than realising which way the wind was blowing, Miller took umbrage at his loyalty to rugby league being questioned – and then attended a conference that hoped to change league into something else.

Talk among delegates at the conference continued, with some suggesting the game could appeal to the Americans as a less-lethal version of their gridiron. At the turn of the century, American football was a deadly sport – it got so bad President Theodore Roosevelt threatened to abolish the game if changes weren't made.

The 1933 push did get one step further than previous attempts in that a game was actually played under universal football rules. Held at Moore Park (now Fox Studios) the 11 August match was a secret endeavour with teams made up of visiting Queensland Aussie rules players supplemented by some local league players. Still, they couldn't get enough for a 15-a-side match and so the trial featured 12 players a side.

The night before the match Miller gave an overview of the rules, which included a comprise on the niggling off-side rule. A soccer-style approach would be taken, where a player was onside as long as there were two defenders between him and the goal.

Despite the week-long efforts to keep the match secret, a Sydney journalist from *The Sun* crept inside to watch the game. He was quite gentle in his report, recognising the match was more to familiarise the players with the rules than to convert any observers.

He liked the off-side approach, saying it allowed players to kick forward 'having the effect of producing the high marks of Australian rules, drawing out defenders to soar into the air with the attacker to get the ball'. The rule that a tackled player had to give the ball to the opposition also got the tick, because it added speed to the game.

The absence of 'the tedious scrum of rugby league' was also a plus, the reporter noted, it being replaced by the umpire bouncing the ball up. For the Australian rules players, there would need to be some practice before they got the rugby league dummy and swerve. 'Particularly this was evident when a league man, streaking for the corner with three or four Australian rules defenders cutting at him across field, side-stepped infield for the try while the Australian rules men, unable to check their career, flashed past him into touch.'

After the trial match, the conference made the decision to create a final draft of the rules and pass them on to the various leagues of existing codes for future consideration. The NSWRL wasted no time in saying 'no thanks', putting an end to talk of universal football just a few days later. Though it was a much closer-run thing than expected. At a league committee meeting, the vote was 15 to 10 against any further consideration of universal football – a few more supporters and there would have been life in the proposed code.

The response from the Australian rules side of the fence suggested there was division over there too. Con Hickey, also chairman of the Australian Football Council, declared disappointment at the NSWRL decision. 'That appears to be the end of it,' he said. 'We can do nothing further.'

But the rugby league decision came as no surprise to the leaders of other Australian rules bodies. NSW Australian Rules League secretary J Allison wasn't surprised nothing came of the plan as it was never going to be an easy thing to implement. 'Personally, I do not think there is a hope of making drastic changes,' he said. 'It must be a matter of evolution, and it will take a matter of 10 years of hard work and hard thinking to get over the matter.

'I certainly think that some of the Australian rules features could be abolished, for instance, do away with the behind posts and substitute a crossbar.

'Introduce the rugby tackle and thus do away with the very fine line of demarcation at present noticeable in the 'hold the ball – hold the man' rule.'

His Australian Rules League president, Mr A Provan, wasn't surprised either. He expected the league to say no. 'Personally I think it was the only natural result,' he said. 'It was obviously too hard for either code to give away so much to make it practical.

'But I will say this – if anyone will be the loser it will be the NSWRL.'

3

A LEAGUE OF THEIR OWN

Since 2018 there has been a national women's rugby league competition, as well as State of Origin fixtures. It even gets a regular slot on TV. But there are still some people who snigger at the idea of women playing rugby league, which is weird because they've had more than a century to get used to the idea.

Despite what they may think, the idea of women playing footy is nothing new. In 1912, league in NSW was just four years old when a woman who signed her name 'Rosella' wrote to the NSWRL secretary Edward Larkin asking him to set up a women's league.

'Don't you think that some good ladies' clubs should be formed and a competition started? We could play before the big matches, and I am sure we would get a lot of exercise, and cause quite a lot of interest to be taken in our game! You should be able to get nearly all the lady runners to play.'

The Sun got a copy of the letter and wrote a story about it, complete with the sort of condescension and sexism that would inevitably follow any talk of female footballers.

'Now there is a chance of seeing the Australian girl careering down the football field, taking a pass, tackling her sylph-like sister, who may be found on the wing,' the reporter wrote, 'or the more corpulent specimen of femininity, whose mission may be to hold the scrum.

'Then may be pictured the weird spectacle of dishevelled hair and the dragging of an excited opponent over the line at the end of it.'

It seems Larkin didn't make any effort to get a league going, so by 1921 the women decided to do it themselves. In June of that year a meeting was held near the NSWRL headquarters, where a women's league was established. The meeting decided five clubs would be formed – Glebe-Balmain, Newtown-South Sydney, North Sydney, Eastern Suburbs and a combined St George-Western Suburbs-University side.

The women were nothing if not ambitious; while several women's matches would take place, there is no record of any of those five teams competing. Later that month, they had their first training session at the Sydney Sports Ground, with most turning up for a run in their bathing suits (the 1921 variety, remember).

The Sun estimated around 100 women turned up. 'There were slim girls, stout girls, squat girls, frail girls, nuggety girls cut out by nature to be halfbacks, and long-limbed girls destined for forwards.' Of course, the reporter couldn't resist being demeaning, describing a scrum full of women as 'scrumptious' and referring to a female player as having 'a lithe, boyish figure.'

The NSW Ladies Rugby Football League secretary Eulalie Stagpoole told the media they had ordered the uniforms – knee-length pants, a jersey and headgear with padded earflaps. Specially made boots were also on the way. Stagpoole made sure people knew they weren't treating this as a novelty. 'We have all followed football from early youth, and love it,' she said. 'All of us prefer rugby [league] and see no reason why we should not play it.'

The first women's league game in Australia was played on 17 September at the Sydney Showground. However, the NSWRL, who seemed surprised the women had actually gotten this far, said any league, club, player or official taking part in the match would be disqualified.

It was a big threat given that none other than Dally Messenger was going to be giving a kicking exhibition at half-time. Officially, the reason was that the game was being privately financed, but it isn't hard to see a degree of sexism behind it.

The women didn't care; on Saturday afternoon teams representing Metropolis and Sydney (basically suburbs versus city) took to the field and played in front of a crowd estimated to be 20,000-strong.

Fifteen-year-old Maggie Maloney caught the spectators' attention, scoring four tries for Metropolis including one that started from her own 25 when she ran around her opposite winger and then beat the fullback to the line. Her efforts saw her make the front page of Monday's *The Sun*, where she was compared to Dally Messenger (who, by the way, ignored the league's disqualification threat and carried out his kicking show).

'It is rumoured that this was not her first match,' *The Sun* reported in a surprisingly detailed and snigger-free article. 'A small kid in boys togs might have been seen playing in the scratch football played in the open spaces near her home in Surry Hills, and practising kicking in back lanes with other youthful football enthusiasts.'

Other papers noted the crowd had come for a joke more than anything else. 'The rival teams, on entering the playing area, were the subject of much ironical laughter, and had to face a battery of cameras,' one paper reported. 'The majority of the crowd had come to jeer but before the match had gone far, their jeers changed to cheers, for the women played real football.'

For the record, Metropolis won 21-11, on the back of Maloney's four-try haul. The Sydney side wasn't happy about losing and asked for a rematch the following week, which was okay with the Metropolis team. So next Saturday they were back at the showground, but this time the crowd had dwindled to 6000.

Sydney got their revenge, winning 9-3. Maloney scored Metropolis' sole try but, as is the way with a player who has a sparkling debut, the Sydney team made sure she was covered during the rematch.

In April and August of 1922, the two sides played exhibition matches in Newcastle – the first was won by Sydney 25-10, with Metropolis squaring the ledger 13-0 in the fourth match.

The two sides met up one more time, in Sydney in October, with the 11-all draw meaning the five-match series ended 2-2. The women's league disbanded in 1923, in part it seems over a dispute as to whether to hire a male secretary.

But that didn't mean the end of women playing rugby league. In 1930 two teams – Metropolis and NSW – travelled from Sydney to Orange for a match at the showground that ended in a draw. The local paper figured they knew why some people would attend the game.

'Of course many people will go through the turnstiles with a mind prejudiced against girls playing football, while others will attend in the hope of having a real laugh, expecting that the girls will be an utter failure on the football field, but writers venture the opinion that these girls will show many of the senior players just how football should be played.'

After the Orange fixture, the two teams played a pair of games against each other in Sydney. Coverage of the game showed perceptions had not been changed, with the Sydney *Daily Pictorial* promoting the Sydney Showground match by stating 'flashing female legs, dimpled knees, powdered noses and bobbed hair will be in abundance.'

In 1931, the women's code made it across the border with a Queensland fixture between Tenterfield and Wallangarra, which was won by Wallangarra 9-3. Two teams played in Orange in 1947, the local paper cringingly writing, 'a couple of the young women are said to weigh in the vicinity of 12 stone [76 kilograms], so they should certainly be able to put a good deal of weight into their actions.'

In August of that year, women representing the Ritz Club and the Telephone Exchange Club played a fundraiser on a muddy Wagga ground for the Food For Britain Appeal. You could hear the Wagga *Daily Advertiser* reporter's sniggering while reading his report of 'one of the most humorous rugby league games ever played.'

'The girls were having fun and games,' he wrote, 'and most of them were getting a mud beauty bath free of charge.'

In 1953, J Duval wrote to the Rockhampton Rugby League asking if a women's match could be played as a curtain-raiser to a Charity Cup fixture later in the year – the league was okay with that, as long as the two teams had the same number of players. The Blues beat the Greens 5-0 on 16 August in what was reported as a spiteful clash. 'Punches were thrown in one incident during the 24-minute match,' one report stated, 'which was marked by fierce tackling.'

In 1954, two women's teams took to the field in Lismore in front of a crowd estimated at around 2000. 'The 16 players amazed the crowd with their knowledge of football, which had been imparted to them by Country Week representatives Mark Patch and Ken O'Reilly,' the *Northern Star* reported. 'The game was played according to the strict rules of the code, although referee Fred Less was at times a little lenient, there were certainly no beg-pardons.'

North Lismore dominated their southern rivals in that match, running out winners 20-nil. And through the years up to the formation of the National Women's Rugby League (NRLW) in 2017, women's matches continued to be played sporadically. So the idea of women playing the game isn't unusual at all – it's been happened for almost as long as the game itself.

4

THE BIG BAN

It's quite common for the league to ban a player for a period of time, whether for on-field or off-field indiscretions. Less common is when the league has to ban two players from the same team at the same time – maybe they were involved in what the league and no one else likes to refer to as a 'melee'. But a whole team?

That's what happened to the Glebe club back in 1917. That season the club had gotten off to a flyer, winning their first five games and looking like a real chance to win their first premiership. But the wheels came off, due to a protest from Annandale – Glebe's Round 1 opponent who was despatched 26-5. This was back in the days of the residency rule; each club had its own territory and if you wanted to play for a particular club, you had to live in their territory. In that first match, Glebe fielded a new signing in Newcastle's Dan Davies. Annandale could hardly have missed him – Davies scored one of Glebe's tries.

The Dales had a problem with Davies – he lived in their district. So the club protested to the league. They had already spoken to the league about Davies, having found him in their district and asked him to play for them. Davies said he would, as long as he wasn't picked for Glebe. At the time Annandale asked the league to decide who he could play for, the league finding in Annandale's favour.

That didn't bother Glebe, who had the audacity to play the player in question against Annandale the following weekend. 'You can plainly see that Annandale had no option but to protest,' the club treasurer by the name of Wilton told *The Arrow* newspaper, 'with the result that Annandale have lost a player that would have no doubt made a big difference to the side.'

For their sins, Davies was banned from playing and Glebe was docked the two points for the win, which started the club's problems. Like some modern-day fans, Glebe figured the league had it in for them. As well as this decision (even if it was justified) Glebe was also unhappy with the treatment of players who had been sent off, including captain Frank Burge in the Round 4 match against Souths and later suspended for two weeks.

A Glebe fan wrote to *The Arrow* complaining about his team's unfair treatment. 'The referees as well as the committee are harsh in their treatment of Glebe,' he wrote, before pointing out how Eastern Suburbs players seemed to be treated more leniently by the judiciary than those from Glebe. In doing so, he showed fans' perception that Eastern Suburbs getting special treatment from the league was nothing new.

'I stated in last Saturday's *Arrow*,' he continued to rant, 'that Glebe had sent more men to the war than any other team, and this is how the controlling league body rewards patriotism! A fine way of appreciating self-sacrifice!'

The straw that broke the camel's back for the Glebe club was the league's decision to move the clash with top-of-the-table

Balmain from the Sydney Cricket Ground (SCG) to Birchgrove Oval. The move stripped from Glebe a share of the big gate expected from staging the game at the SCG. And so the players chose to boycott the match.

'There is no disguising the fact that the Glebe club and supporters of the game in the district consider that they have strong grievances against rugby league,' *The Arrow* reported. 'The disqualification of the club in the Annandale match, the disqualification of players sent off the field while some belonging to other clubs have been merely censured, and the placing of the Balmain match at Birchgrove Reserve are causes of discontent.'

The league wasted no time in responding; a day after Glebe's announcement, it took the jaw-dropping step of suspending all 14 players who took part in the boycott, outing them until the end of the following season. 'It is considered that they have flouted the authority of the league,' reported *The Arrow*, 'and that only drastic action can meet the case in order that nothing of the kind shall happen again.'

Glebe continued its fight against the league, noting that two of the suspended players weren't going to play anyway, and a third was already suspended for the rest of the season for an earlier offence. And yet those three players were now out until the first round of the 1919 season.

That is, unless the league had a change of heart. Which it did – to a degree. In April of the following year, just a month before the start of the 1918 season, the suspended players appealed against the suspension. The league found it in their hearts to lift the suspension on all but two players, captain Frank Burge and his brother Alby. There appear to be no news reports on why the pair were treated differently, though it couldn't have helped the club's belief the league was persecuting them. However, a week later, the suspension of Frank was lifted in time for Round 1 against Annadale. Alby had to wait another week before the league allowed him to return to Glebe.

The team would be competitive for the 1918 season – finishing third – and for several seasons thereafter. In 1922 they finished equal first. With the competition awarded to whoever was top of the table at the end of the season, a tie meant a play-off was called for. So on a Wednesday afternoon, four days after the final round, Glebe played Norths for the title and lost 35-3.

For the rest of the decade, the side was up and down and, on 31 August 1929, it played its last regular season match – a 24-all draw against North Sydney. But Glebe didn't know the significance of the game at the time. The league's axe would fall on the club well into the off-season.

In September, with the competition awaiting a NSWRL boundaries commission report, there was talk that Glebe would have to merge with Balmain. Some suggested the merged club be called Dally, in honour of Dally Messenger. However, the commission instead recommended that Glebe be kicked out altogether.

Not surprisingly, the club was quite unimpressed by this recommendation. 'My club is not going to take this lying down,' said Glebe secretary Eric Lloyd. 'Our district has been greatly disadvantaged by the industrialisation of a once-popular residential area. My club has maintained its traditions against odds, and my officials feel that the boundaries committee would have been wiser and fairer in giving us more territory rather than wiping us out.'

On 11 November, the league chose to wipe out one of its foundation clubs – but it was a close-run thing with the final vote only just getting up 13-12. Petitions with thousands of signatures and delegations of local councillors had not been able to sway the league.

'The proposal had caused consternation and the people of the district were up in arms,' *The Sun* reported, showing supporters' passion for their team has always been a part of league. 'They had looked upon the Glebe team as their baby and whether in victory or defeat they had a high regard for the club. A grievous injury would be done if it was eliminated.'

Glebe secretary Lloyd had hit the nail on the head when he spoke of the area's increasing industrialisation. That was part of the reason for ousting the team; the population of the area had remained static for several years with the factories moving in forcing residents to move out – reducing the club's supporter base. The league didn't help matters by refusing to let Glebe renew a lease on the league-owned Wentworth Park. Not getting the price it wanted from Glebe, the league took the bizarre step of leasing the ground to a rival code – soccer. So not only would the league axe Glebe's rugby league side, they would also invite a competitor into the district.

In an echo of the campaign launched when South Sydney were kicked out of the comp in 2000, the remaining residents of Glebe decided to fight back. In mid-November a public meeting was arranged at the Glebe Town Hall to protest their team's exclusion, with fans packing out the venue.

'There was no mistaking the mighty "aye" that shook the rafters and echoed like a challenge through the musty corridors of the Glebe Town Hall last night,' reported *The Sun*. 'Backs and forwards, their fathers and their sweethearts rose to their feet and cheered. With one voice they registered an emphatic protest against the exclusion of the Glebe club from district league matches and expressed the hope that the decision will be reversed on Monday night.'

Monday night was when the league's general committee was due to meet. On the table was a recission motion moved by St George delegate J Mostyn on the decision to kick out Glebe. Using the electoral rolls as evidence, he suggested instead giving Glebe some area from Western Suburbs, South Sydney and Newtown to strengthen the club.

Obviously those three clubs were opposed to the motion; South Sydney noting the part of its territory proposed to go to Glebe was where most of their players lived. The vote to erase the decision to boot out Glebe was 12-12, but a three-fifths majority was needed to overturn a boundaries committee decision, so the club remained on the outer.

But they weren't quite done with the fighting. In February, Glebe officials made a concerted effort to take over Balmain by running for positions on the black-and-golds board. Balmain responded by protesting to the league that some Glebe members likely to vote at the annual meeting were not paid-up Balmain members.

The league, likely wishing Glebe would just quietly go away, asked Balmain to take quite a liberal view as to membership. In the end, the key positions were filled by Balmain people, scuppering any plans the Glebe contingent – some of whom made the club committee – may have had.

A month out from the start of the 1930 season, there were still some rough spots. Balmain only saw fit to take on 14 former Glebe players across all three grades. Also, Balmain officials claimed those in charge at Glebe had been doing something shonky when it came to the residency rules.

'Numerous examples of old addresses that fit in with the district requirements being retained when the persons have moved to other localities are being investigated,' wrote *The Sydney Sportsman*, 'and in several cases prominent players' places of residence are unknown.'

At the end of the day, the league was able to get Balmain officials to stop carrying on in time for the start of the season. However, having so much of Glebe's territory didn't help Balmain in 1930 – they finished sixth with just five wins.

THE GAME COULD NOT BE CALLED SPECTACULAR, AND THERE WAS A CONFUSION OF COLOURS.

5

FOOTBALL UNDER LIGHTS

For many, rugby league under lights began in the 1970s with the mid-week Amco Cup where Sydney teams joined with rep sides from country NSW regions to slap black goo under their eyes and play four-quarter footy.

But the concept of night footy started a long time before then – the first games were way back in 1928. They caused a bit of controversy too, with the NSWRL threatening to disqualify any players who took the field.

The concept began in Newcastle with a game on 29 November 1928, at the speedway in Hamilton. 'The lighting system on the ground made it possible to follow the progress of the play with unexpected clearness,' reported The *Northern Star*, 'and the white painted ball was easily visible whenever kicked or passed.'

With as many as 52 players from the Newcastle rugby league competition taking part, the local league had concerns it wouldn't be good for them. They feared it would spark a rival summer code, and voiced their concerns to the head office in Sydney.

A night match between 1928 premiers Souths and runners-up Easts was planned for Sydney in early December, with officials from both clubs not sanctioning the match but not objecting to players taking part.

That feeling changed once they heard the complaint from the Newcastle committee, which had suggested that Sydney players could pack up and move to the town each summer to play in the new competition. As an example, the finger was pointed at St George fullback Frank Meighan, who had just moved to Newcastle. He actually had to explain himself, stating the railways had moved his job there for a few months, though he hoped to be back before the winter of 1929.

'League authorities are not regarding the innovation seriously,' the *Telegraph* reported, 'but some of them are strongly opposed to the institution of a competition, and will move at the next meeting of the league that organised competitions under such conditions should not be countenanced.'

'As an exhibition match I feel that the league would not interfere,' said NSWRL secretary Horrie Miller, 'but if a competition is the idea behind the preliminary, the league would not be prepared to hand the control of the game to an outside body.'

The Souths versus Easts fixture at the Sydney Showground would have to share the stage with a series of motorcycle races – the game was organised by the speedway promoter. It was scheduled for 15 December, with games split into 20-minute halves and each side cut down to nine players. That meant only three forwards per side would take the field, so as to give the public a better view of the ball in the scrum. Another rule change saw a team given a point if the opposition kicked the ball out on the full, as did knocking the ball over the dead-ball line.

In the lead-up to the Sydney fixture night games continued at Newcastle, further putting the wind up the NSWRL. When heavy rain delayed the Sydney match until 22 December, the league had time to mull over their response, which was harsh. The body barred its players from taking part and threatened to disqualify any who ignored the order.

That didn't seem to worry most of the players, who felt they were duty-bound to honour their commitment to play the night game. 'We feel that we would be doing the greater wrong by not playing,' said Easts' Les Steel. 'We promised to play and the match would have been held last Saturday night but for the rain. The officials at headquarters raised no objection until the Newcastle case was introduced. This is only a novelty – not a match under the jurisdiction or control of the league.'

On game day, Easts were still keen but Souths started to get cold feet, only agreeing to take part after a conference of team managers. Still, several players decided not to play: Souths' top pointscorer that year Benny Wearing, Test player George Treweek and forward Eddie Root. On the tricolours' side, only Joe Busch stood down.

'The ground was brilliantly lighted with floodlights and the ball was enamelled white,' the Sydney *Truth* match report noted. 'The game could not be called spectacular, and there was a confusion of colours. It was hard to distinguish the players and the exhibition lacked the brilliancy of the sunlight game.'

Souths beat their grand final opponents again, with the scoreline reading 10-6. The league ordered all the players to appear before a committee to explain why they shouldn't be disqualified. They offered the explanation that the league's disqualification threat had been issued too late for them to honourably withdraw from the game. Showing the threat was an empty one, the league accepted their excuse and allowed them to play in the 1929 season.

Events were a bit more heated in Newcastle, where the night football competition began. Several committee members who had been involved in organising the floodlit games ended up resigning.

No night games of rugby league were played the following summer. Though the NSWRL would eventually grab hold of this night football concept, staging a few matches of its own in 1933. That summer, after the season had finished, University played Western Suburbs and St George met up with Newtown in a double-header at the showground on 23 October. Further games were to follow in November, with the final held on 11 November. St George was the winner of the first-ever official night football competition, defeating North Sydney 16-6.

6

THE WORST TEAM EVER

When it comes to the question of the worst rugby league side in the national competition, there are certainly no shortage of contenders. In their final standalone season in 1999, the Western Suburbs Magpies weren't much chop. They took out the wooden spoon, winning just three games and losing 21. The black-and-whites let in an astonishing 944 points at an average of 39 points a game. Their opponents broke the half-century on seven occasions, including Penrith 60-6, Brisbane 50-0, 68-10 against Parramatta and 60-16 against Auckland.

Maybe it's the Illawarra Steelers of 1985-86. They finished last in those two seasons, winning just 12 of 48 matches over that period. But they didn't get flogged like Wests.

In 1993 the Gold Coast Seagulls could only score a single win out of their 24 games. The unlucky opponent? The Newcastle Knights, who lost 22-6.

At least those teams managed to win a game or two. The 1966 Eastern Suburbs Roosters went through that year without a single win. Their opponents racked up an average score of 24 points per game and their biggest loss was a 53-0 effort against Manly. Back in those days, 53 points was a ridiculously high score given tries were worth three points then. With 11 tries scored, in modern-day figures, Manly scored 64 points.

The Souths squad of 1946 also went through winless. In its debut year of 1935, Canterbury-Bankstown managed to be on the wrong side of the two biggest winning margins in league history – in successive weeks. In a fortnight, the scoreboard read 178-13.

But to find some truly awful sides, you have to go further back in time. In its last years in the competition Annadale really stunk up the place. From 1917 to 1920 when they pulled the pin, Annandale finished last each year (though in the interests of accuracy, they were equal last in 1917 and 1919). Throughout those four years, the side won just two games – one in 1917 (there were also two draws that season) and one in 1919. In 1920 they were held to nil in four matches. Overall, they played 55 games for just two wins and three draws over those four years.

However, the ignominious honour of the worst team ever has to go to University who, in the period between 1929 and 1938 managed to string together a quartet of wooden spoons – *twice.* The bright spot in that cavalcade of misery was the 1933 season when they managed to win a surprising five games and finished second last.

The team began in 1920 as a direct challenge to the traditional rugby union stronghold of Sydney University. The rival code had been struggling to regain the strength it had prior to World War I, after it paused the competition during the war years. So the league saw a chance to kill off union. 'A strong league club has been formed at the university because the men believed it was the better game of rugby,' the *Rugby League News* reported in 1920. 'The old cry that boys leaving the Great Public Schools, if they played league football would not be able to do so at the university would now be a thing of the past.'

The club didn't start well, winning just one game in their first season and none in their second, managing to string together five in 1922. Easily their best season was in 1926 when they won nine of their first 11 games to be sitting in second spot come Round 12. A late-season slump saw them lose their last five matches, but the good work early in the season was enough to see them finish fourth and make the finals. In an indication of how far ahead University was, they managed to remain in second spot for almost all of their losing slump, only slipping to fourth with the last-round defeat at the hands of Souths.

In the semi-final against Glebe, they managed to rediscover their form, handing out a 29-3 pasting. That put them into the final against top-of-the-table Souths, who had defeated them in both regular season matches. University was the sentimental favourite 'because of the clean and open football they play'. And also because everyone loves an underdog – well, except for those who support the underdog's opponent.

According to match reports of the final, that clean, open play wasn't in evidence. 'There was an attendance of 21,000 lured to the Agricultural Ground in anticipation of a brilliant exhibition of football, of which both teams are capable on their day,' reported *The Sun*. 'There was a big disappointment in store. Never at any stage did the match reach the heights of brilliance.'

In a dour, hard defensive game, the underdog was always behind and lost 11-5.

Aside from just missing out on the finals in 1928 by just one win, the general trajectory for University from that bright spot in 1926 was all downhill. They only avoided the wooden spoon once between 1929 and 1937. That their regular position was at the bottom of the ladder wasn't really a surprise. University was really up against it when trying to be successful in the competition. The players had amateur status, while their opponents were paid to play, and the club had no home ground for its entire existence. The students, fresh from school, were rushed into the top grade, where they had to do battle against older, match-hardened players. They would also lose players when they graduated, or see their top talent poached by other sides with the lure of cash.

For most of that last decade, University had the worst attack and worst defence in the league. In 1930 they averaged just eight points a game while letting in 22 – certainly not any sort of recipe for success. Their final year was even worse, scoring just five points a game but leaking 38. That year saw the team on the wrong side of some real thumpings: 63-0 to Souths to start the season, 48-3 to Newtown, 65-5 at the hands of St George and 53-8 at North Sydney.

No wonder the team decided to call it quits. Before the club's last match – against Canterbury in the now-defunct post-season City Cup tournament – officials told the league not to expect to see them go round again in 1938. Club official F Benning told the league in the days before that match against Canterbury at Belmore they were done and asked for an unusual favour. The club wanted to forfeit the third-grade match, so that two teams of old University players could have one last run-around. 'In view of the performances of University this year,' he said, 'we realise what may happen and old players want to make sure they will be there at the finish.' The league agreed to the request, as long as University didn't do something sneaky like turning up to play the following year.

The league itself had a few good reasons for wanting to see the back of University. With them gone it would bring the competition back to an even eight teams, which would remove the need for a bye and thereby make creating a draw much easier. Also, University was such a poor performer that people wouldn't pay to see them play, meaning home teams actually ended up out of pocket. 'Teams like Eastern Suburbs, South Sydney and Canterbury-Bankstown have lost financially this season on matches against University,' reported the *Telegraph*, 'gatemen's wages and other expenses exceeding the receipts.'

In the last game of the winless 1937 season the top-grade University side went down 13-2 to Canterbury in a match marred by heavy rain. At the end of the game, the two sides swapped jerseys. And, true to their word, University didn't return.

TWO OF THE THREE FOOTBALLS USED IN THE GAME WERE MADE OF RUBBER.

7

FORTNIGHT OF FLOGGINGS

The worst fortnight in rugby league history must surely belong to the 1935 Canterbury-Bankstown side. It was their first season in the competition, and they managed to scratch together just two wins – both against the perpetually ordinary University side (though they only just won one of those matches 16-15). The new boys finished second-last on the ladder, leaking in a season-worst 41 points a game.

It was a season full of shellackings: 37-9 in Round 2 against Souths, 44-5 the week after against Balmain, 49-9 against Newtown, 65-11 at the hands of Wests and a 65-10 loss to Easts at the back end of the season.

But the worst of it happened in rounds 5 and 6, where Canterbury-Bankstown managed to concede the two biggest losing margins in league history in successive weeks. And those embarrassing records still stand and are unlikely to ever be beaten. In Round 5, they came up against St George – a team that would finish just one place higher on the ladder (albeit also 12 points ahead) at the end of the season – at Earl Park. To be fair, the blue-and-whites probably shouldn't have bothered to turn up.

The Red V handed Canterbury a still-unfathomable 91-6 defeat. And to make it even more unfathomable, Canterbury led 4-0 at the 20-minute mark, meaning St George poured on 91 points in an hour – 68 of them in the second half. Remember that tries were worth three points back then. In today's money, Saints' scoreline would have been 110.

Justifiably, the *Truth* newspaper really laid in the boots after Canterbury's performance. 'Whoever told the hyphenates they could play football is the world's greatest leg-puller. But the joke's on rugby league for accepting a combination that would be towelled by a team of salmon-tin dribblers. And they're fixing up a brand-new ground for them. What for? To use for kiss-in-the-ring, or just to gambol about like lambs in the spring?'

It wasn't just the highest score in a game of first-grade league. It was also the first time all 13 players in a team got on the scoreboard and kicker Les Griffin got the single-scorer record with a 30-point haul. He also took the record for most goals in a match with 15.

But that kicking record might need to come with an asterisk, because two of the three footballs used in the game were made of rubber – which may have assisted somewhat in goal kicking. St George had used them in trial matches but this was the first time they had appeared in an official fixture (they had tried to use them a week earlier against University but the opponents' captain objected).

A few days after the game, the league met to decide on the legality of the rubber ball. 'Our players do complain,' Canterbury-Bankstown secretary F Miller said, 'that it is too lively and the bounce beats them.' Though, when you get flogged 91-6 you're going to look for any excuse. At any rate, the league decided the balls had to be the same across all games and so banned any further use of the rubber ball. Which was fine with St George, whose players weren't bothered either way.

Excuses about the ball wouldn't be able to mitigate against the scoreline the following Saturday at the Sydney Sports Ground against Easts. That season's eventual premiers thumped the newcomers 87-7, coming within a whisker of breaking what a week ago must have seemed like an unassailable record score. Easts certainly had their chance to score more than 91 points; they actually got off to a slow start. The first half scoreline was just 37-2, meaning Easts scored 50 points in one half of footy.

There were records set the previous week that were broken in this game. Griffin got to hang onto his single-game pointscoring record for all of seven days. Easts' centre and captain Dave Brown took it off his hands with a 45-point haul in the form of five tries and 15 goals. He would have broken Griffin's record that year anyway in the Easts-Canterbury rematch later in the 1935 season, where he scored 38 of Easts' 65 points (for the record the St George-Canterbury rematch in 1935 was a less-embarrassing 34-6).

Canterbury-Bankstown proved to be quick learners, however. The following season they made the finals – beating St George and drawing with Easts that year. In 1938, they finished as minor premiers. The blue-and-whites had the best attack and best defence that year, and handed out a few beatings of their own, including a first-round 33-5 victory over Norths.

They also had the sweet revenge of defeating Eastern Suburbs 19-6 in the final to claim the premiership.

‘THIS GAME WILL PUT THE LEAGUE BACK 20 YEARS. I’VE NEVER SEEN FIRST GRADERS IN A FINAL PLAY SO POORLY.’

8

FIXING THE GAME?

In the 1943 season three Newtown players said they had been offered bribes to throw a match. Second rower Herb Narvo, centre Des Fullerton and halfback Tom Nevin claimed they had been offered cash by bookies to have a bad game against Balmain in Round 10.

Fullerton said he was approached by a man he had never met before who was an agent for a bookmaker. 'He offered me the odds of £30 if Newtown lost to Balmain the following afternoon,' he said. 'I told him to go away or I would call the police. I reported the matter to the Newtown committee.' As halfback, Nevin had more control over the game and so was offered £50 to 'play crook'. Narvo, who was a boxer, and later heavyweight champ, said he wisely refrained from punching the bookie out after also being offered £50.

The final scoreline showed the Newtown side didn't run dead – the ladder leaders and eventual premiers walloped the third-placed Balmain 35-7, with Narvo and Fullerton both scoring tries.

Gambling on the footy was increasingly of concern for the league, though they appeared to do very little with the news of players being offered money to throw a game. With widespread betting taking place on that Newtown-Balmain game, the league just put it down to the fact there were no horse races that weekend – voting 21-2 to take no action.

'The raceless Saturday is to blame,' crowed the league's deputy chairman Frank Miller. 'Bookmakers are at a loose end and attend the football, not to watch but to bet.'

The situation was the same in the minor premiership play-off between the two teams in August. 'I estimate that £10,000 will be at stake on the game,' one Randwick bookmaker told the *Telegraph*. 'One of my regular clients wanted to back Newtown to win him £500.' Newtown secretary Dave Jolly said he regretted 'the betting orgy' but claimed 'there is nothing the clubs – or the league – can do about it.'

Come the final Newtown was favourite over North Sydney despite not having beaten them in three matches that season. After having scored a total of 31 points across those three games, Newtown managed to rack up more in the season decider to win 34-7.

Those concerns about betting on Newtown games, and the rumours of players being paid to throw games came up again in the finals of the 1944 season. This was back in the era when, if the minor premiers were defeated in the post-season, they had the right to challenge the winner of the final – in a game that was called the grand final.

In 1944, Newtown had again finished as minor premiers and thumped St George 55-7 in the semis. That brought them up against Balmain (again) in the final after the Tigers got over Souths 15-6. There was a lot of interest in the match; the State

Government even put on special trams from Circular Quay and Central Station to the SCG.

In a surprise result, Balmain took the game 19-16 after being down 11-0 after the first 20 minutes. That triggered the mandatory rematch – and more than a few people thought something was suss. In the game, Newtown goal kicker Tom Kirk had a shocker. The player who had scored 185 points and kicked 88 goals – including a massive 11 in that semi against St George – missed three easy goals including one from in front of the sticks. Spectators – those who didn't walk out of the SCG before full time – bemoaned the poor standard of play and the general lethargy of some of those in a Newtown jersey.

'I still can't work it out,' pondered Newtown coach Arthur Folwell. 'The forwards couldn't raise a gallop and the backs missed easy passes.' Former international and St George official Arthur 'Snowy' Justice was disgusted by what he saw. 'This game will put the league back 20 years. I've never seen first graders in a final play so poorly.' Newtown captain Frank Farrell hit back at the jeering from the crowd, insisting his team 'were definitely flat out' and noted they were without several key players.

The result stoked rumours that the result had been fixed by bookies, with the odds swinging sharply and suddenly in Balmain's favour the day of the game. The league also gave consideration to scrapping the right for minor premiers to challenge because, as in this instance, it created a dead rubber. Newtown could have afforded to lose the final because they were able to demand a rematch the following week.

And that's just what a segment of the football public figured had happened. Though not because the players had been bribed, but because Newtown had plotted to lose the final so as to get another hit of cash from the takings of the grand final. Officials from both sides refuted the claims that Newtown went easy on Balmain. 'People seem to have lost sight of the fact that Balmain had twice beaten stronger Newtown teams in the two rounds of the competition,' said Balmain's Harold Matthews. 'There was no suggestion of anything wrong on those occasions.'

Newtown's Jolly was outraged that some officials were questioning the character of players. 'Not for a moment do I suspect that any of our players did not try. I blame the whole thing on some league officials for making statements for which they had no justification. When the minor premiers in the rugby union and Australian rules were beaten, officials of those organisations did not cast reflections on the defeated players.'

He went in all guns blazing at a league meeting the following day, alleging some of the officials had been punting on the game. 'I really believe that the worst evil we have got in this code at the present time is not the possibility of a footballer not giving of his best in a game, but the very near possibility of officials delving into gambling activities,' he said. 'In most cases a loss makes them speak through their pockets.'

Despite – or perhaps because of – this criticism, the league committee passed a motion expressing confidence in the integrity of the players in the final. Snowy Justice himself put forward a motion that the grand final gate be donated to charity in the hope it would regain the public's confidence – no one would even second it and so it went no further.

He again called for the grand final challenge to be scrapped, but didn't get that across the line either. Others said if the league moved that way, it would be tantamount to saying there was in fact something wrong in the Newtown-Balmain game.

The *Telegraph* was critical of the league's head-in-the-sand approach to betting, stating 'club officials are among the code's heaviest betters'. It brought up the previous season's alarming news of attempts to entice Newtown players to throw a game, noting the league's less than encouraging response. 'The league didn't even question the players,' the *Telegraph* said. 'The matter was discussed behind closed doors and the president [Harry Flegg] refused to make a statement to press. At least three of the rugby league general committee knew who were responsible for approaching the players. They kept a discreet silence.'

For the grand final, the police would send members of the gambling squad to watch out for betting – including those handing out 'doubles', which are sealed cards that contain the names of one player for each team. If those players are the first scorers, the card holder wins.

One flaw in the claim that Newtown threw the final is that the side needed to be quite sure it would win the rematch. And that didn't happen – Balmain beat them again, 12-8, this time in heavy rain and driving winds. 'Wild statements that last week's match was rigged made us try all the harder today,' Balmain captain Arthur Patton said. 'It was a hard game, but not as tough as the final.' It was surely small comfort to the

Newtown side that Balmain centre Joe Jorgenson missed a goal from an easier position than Kirk had a week earlier. 'It showed once more to those who think they know all that the best kicker can sometimes fail,' wrote *The Sun*'s Claude Corbett.

9

BUMPER AND THE EAR BITE

It was pretty obvious St George front rower Bill McRitchie would have something coming his way when they played Newtown for the second time in the 1945 season. In the Round 6 match, McRitchie collected Newtown captain Frank Farrell with a high tackle that snapped off four of his teeth at the gumline. At least this was the claim Newtown's Charles 'Chicka' Cahill made years later – none of the contemporary newspaper reports of the game make any mention of a bloodied Farrell.

So when the Dragons headed to Henson Park in late July for the return bout, McRitchie must have been preparing for a get-square from the man they called Bumper.

Likely he was looking for something like a stiff-arm or maybe a sneaky uppercut delivered under the cover of the scrum. Having a good part of his ear chomped on and left on the turf wouldn't have been something he was preparing for. But that's what happened – allegedly. To this day there is dispute about what actually happened; some say Farrell bit him in a scrum, others claim there was only a small tear and McRitchie made it worse by tugging at it. Farrell himself insisted to his dying day that he never bit down, noting that his false teeth were in the shed at the time (much, much later, perhaps sick of all the questions, he would falsely claim he never played the game in question).

Newtown were riding high in second spot when the Dragons came to Henson Park, while the visitors were down in second-last place. Newtown won the match 23-11, though the result would be overshadowed by what happened when a scrum packed down early in the first half. McRitchie reeled out of the scrum, yelling at Farrell, who had packed down opposite him, before falling to the ground clutching his right ear. He tried to play on but other players, concerned about the amount of blood flowing out, recommended he leave the field. Media reports from the day of the match said most of his lobe and part of the side of the ear had disappeared.

He went to hospital but the wound was so severe that doctors couldn't stitch it up. Instead McRitchie required plastic surgery, which was expected to see him in hospital for eight weeks. The league agreed to foot all his medical bills, a generous offer it would come to regret when McRitchie ended up staying in hospital for most of the remainder of 1945.

The St George player immediately alleged he had been bitten but initially declined to point the finger at anyone. 'The Newtown player sank his teeth into my ear without warning,' he said. 'There had been normal rough and tumble between us but nothing vicious. When he bit me all I knew was to break away in desperation. I think I even scratched his face.' Referee George Bishop immediately told Farrell, 'if I catch you, you'll get life!'

After the game, Newtown official Dave Jolly quickly went into denial mode, offering the ludicrous defences that McRitchie's ear could have been torn by hands, or even caused by someone's foot. How a foot could cause such an injury in a scrum wasn't explained.

In early August, McRitchie named the biter in an affidavit read in a secret league inquiry into the incident. Despite the apparent secrecy, word got out the next day that Farrell was the alleged perpetrator, prompting the police officer to issue a rebuttal denying the allegation. 'No player can truthfully accuse me of biting,' he said. 'I have never resorted to such tactics. I have always endeavoured to play hard, solid football as it should be played, for the benefit of my club and clubmates of the league in general.

'I fail to see why I should be the victim of such adverse criticism about an incident that has no foundation whatsoever.'

In evidence to the inquiry, doctors who saw McRitchie's injury couldn't give a definitive explanation as to what caused it. Referee Bishop was also not helpful, noting that he was on the other side of the scrum to McRitchie and Farrell and could not offer any information about the incident. However, his on-field remarks about Farrell risking a life ban suggested he had a strong opinion as to what had occurred.

Jolly continued his less-than-convincing defence of Farrell, further elaborating on how he felt McRitchie's injury had occurred – no matter that they were more than a little far-fetched. 'I believe that there are two possible causes,' he said, 'either of which could have occurred during a scrum. One is that a Newtown player accidentally wrenched part of McRitchie's ear off with his hand.

'It could be done easily. I am only a small man but I'm sure I could drag the side of a man's ear off. The other possibility is that the injury was caused by a kick from the aluminium stops on a player's boot.'

With McRitchie still in hospital, his arm strapped to his ear in the process of grafting skin onto the injury, on August 29, the league decided to adjourn the inquiry until he could attend in person. On that last day of the inquiry, there was some explosive evidence delivered by St George lock James Hale. The captain alleged he had seen Farrell spitting blood as McRitchie walked from the field. The other Dragons prop in the scrum, Dick Healy, said that after the scrum broke he could see a piece of flesh on the ground. 'One of the opposite players said, "there's a piece of somebody there". I kicked it over with my foot.' On the same day, Farrell again insisted he was not guilty of the charges.

That adjournment did not sit well with the St George club, who felt the league was simply hoping the whole thing would just go away. 'My club is convinced that certain high officials of the NSWRL are using every endeavour to prevent any finality being reached in this matter,' club official Clem Madden stated.

Still in hospital in November having undergone six grafting operations, McRitchie was considering giving up the game, saying 'my career has been one long chapter of injuries since I first played with St George'. In his debut season in 1942 he fractured his ribs, damaged a hip the year after and broke his arm early in 1944. Not surprisingly, his wife was keen for him to give up, suggesting she would make sure he took up a safer sport, like tennis.

That month, Newtown's Herb Narvo said he was planning to transfer to St George for the next season, but denied it was due to the ear-biting incident. There had been rumours Narvo and Farrell fought over the incident. Narvo missed the next two games for Newtown but played in the local league when he went back home to Newcastle. The *Telegraph* claimed the word was he wouldn't return while a certain player was in the team. 'It is stated that he challenged a fellow player in the dressing room after the St George match and told club officials he would not be associated with the side while that player was a member of it.'

Narvo later denied any such incident occurred – and he did return in time to play for Newtown in the semi-final against Balmain, where Farrell was captain. He also returned there in 1949 while that 'fellow player' was still in the team.

Farrell was concerned about his future in the police force if he was found guilty, having faced a departmental inquiry about the incident before the league made its final decision. McRitchie alleged Farrell visited him in hospital and asked him not to pursue the allegations any further for fear it would cost him his job – a claim Farrell denied.

It wasn't until February that the NSWRL inquiry could resume. In a secret ballot rather than the usual show of hands, delegates voted 15 to 12 to clear Farrell of the charges. 'I'm glad it's over,' he said. 'It has been a worrying time.' In his defence Farrell was less than convincing, and sometimes simply dishonest. He told the inquiry that he had packed down on the inside of McRitchie and therefore could not have bitten his right ear – which was refuted by both the St George prop and the referee. Further, he said he couldn't have bitten him anyway because his false teeth were in the dressing sheds – which was true but they were only a few of his top teeth, Farrell still had a row of bottom teeth in his head. Additionally, it was later revealed that Farrell had a party trick of crushing walnuts between his gums, which suggests his jaw would have easily had the strength to deal with McRitchie's ear.

In the St George annual report of 1946, it said the league wanted to be done with the unsavoury incident. 'League officials wanted it dropped quickly and this they did as soon as the decision was reached. They were not concerned with who caused the injury. Far from it! Their decision to vote by secret ballot, and the lack of comment by a majority of the vice-presidents, proved that.'

Cahill, who claimed McRitchie had knocked out the Newtown captain's teeth earlier in the season, suggested the Dragon actually ripped off his own ear.

'I honestly believe that he got his ear torn off with a fingernail,' he told league historian Sean Fagan. 'You know, if you hit somebody on the side of the head with your hand and you grapple over the ear with a fingernail if you had any sort of fingernail, you could tear the bloody skin.

'The piece of skin that came away was about a quarter of an inch wide and I'd say about three-quarters of an inch to an inch long and it was hanging from his ear. One of the St George players said to him "your ear is torn". He put up his hand and pulled it off himself.'

With the protagonists all passed away, the truth of what happened to McRitchie's ear will never be known, though there was no plausible alternate explanation for McRitchie's injury and Farrell's evasiveness when giving evidence is a red flag. What is known is that match against Newtown was McRitchie's last; he opted to take up cricket instead of tennis. As for Farrell, he played six more seasons, retiring in 1951. He also played for Australia after the incident, three times in 1946 and once in 1948. He was also picked for NSW in that time, suggesting he felt no repercussions from selectors after the incident.

EASTERN SUBURBS OFFICIALS WERE SURE THEIR CAPTAIN WOULD PUT THE CLUB BEFORE THE FIGHT. THEY WERE WRONG.

10

FOOTY FIGHTERS

These days it's not unheard of for a league player to try his hand in the boxing ring. But none of them have ever played while being a national title holder. Nor have any of them backed up and played footy the day after a title fight.

That's what forward Herb Narvo did. Narvo played for Newtown for five years (1937, 1943–1945 and 1949) and a year as captain/coach with St George (1946). In between he played for various country sides. While playing for the Bluebags, in 1943 Narvo grabbed the Australian heavyweight title, knocking out Billy 'Wocko' Britt in 45 seconds. He was able to successfully defend that title several times, before losing it to Jack Johnson (not the Galveston Giant, another Jack Johnson) in 1945. While that wasn't a title bout, he lost his belt because he was knocked out and the rules at the time said if you knock out the champ, you get their belt.

On 6 April 1946, a week before the start of the season, Narvo had a rematch with Johnson. It wasn't an issue that St George had a trial against Canterbury the next day, Narvo was going to be at Belmore Oval. 'Football is my profession,' he said, 'and Sunday will be my last chance to have a run with the team before the competition begins the following Saturday.'

He even had a plan to quickly increase his weight from the 85kg needed for the fight to his playing weight of 97kg – beer. He planned on drinking three beers a day for several weeks to increase his weight.

For the fight, it seemed Narvo had God on his side. Ten-year-old schoolboy Geoffrey Cromack had been praying that Narvo would win ever since the fighter-footballer gave him an autograph a week before the bout. It doesn't seem that God was listening to little Geoffrey; Johnson knocked out Narvo in the fifth, after the St George player had already hit the canvas twice in the fourth.

In the fifth round, Johnson hit him with a left to the body and then a sharp one to the jaw as Narvo was falling. The knockout saw Narvo retire from boxing, and he walked away with £400 from the ticket sales – the equivalent of $30,000 in today's money. Not bad for a night's work.

And Narvo made the trial against Canterbury on Sunday. Though he was replaced early in the second half in a match where several St George players complained that they were victims of stiff-arms from Canterbury. St George lost the trial 22-14 though it wasn't an accurate barometer of the Red V's chances. That season, they finished in top spot, only to blow the chance to snare their second premiership by losing to Balmain in the semi-final and again in the grand final challenge.

Narvo was also fighting other players in the ring long before the likes of Paul Gallen and Sonny Bill Williams. In 1942, he went up against fellow international and Eastern Suburbs captain Ray Stehr twice. Narvo won the first bout, though some spectators were left underwhelmed. 'They have played football when they have been out on their feet,' wrote *The Sun*'s WF Corbett. 'But Stehr could not stand up to a cuffing Narvo gave him at Leichhardt Stadium last night. Much to the joy of some partisan folk, he was counted out in the second round.'

The *Telegraph* saw it differently, praising Narvo's knockout. 'It was one of the most spectacular blows seen in Sydney,' the paper reported. 'Narvo, knocked down by Stehr, sprang from a sitting position to floor his opponent. Narvo had rested until the count of 'eight' and rose unexpectedly to deliver the knockout blow. The blow was a left hook, and Stehr fell like a log.'

There must have been some interest in fighting footballers because a Newcastle promoter signed the pair up for a rematch in the steel town in August. At the time, Narvo was playing in the Newcastle comp, but Stehr was signed with Eastern Suburbs, who had a final-round match against St George on the Saturday afternoon before the fight that evening.

Eastern Suburbs officials were sure their captain would put the club before the fight. They were wrong – unbelievably, Stehr pulled out of the match so he could fight Narvo again. It wasn't a meaningless match either; with Easts sitting in third spot a win against St George would guarantee a finals position. A loss along with results of other games going against Easts would see them fall out of the top four.

As it was, Easts lost to St George but managed to sneak into the finals in fourth, just a point ahead of Souths. And the fight was a fizzer too; Stehr lost to a technical knockout after he claimed his hand had been injured and he couldn't continue.

Bear in mind that he had been knocked down seven times in the first three rounds, so the injured hand may have just been an excuse to avoid a real knockout.

Not surprisingly, Eastern Suburbs fans vented their frustrations at Stehr missing the St George match. 'His non-appearance with his team yesterday brought forth wrathful comments,' the *Truth* reported, 'with verbal embellishments from club supporters who reckoned his leaving the team in the lurch, just when they wanted him the most, was not playing the game.'

Oddly enough, that story from the *Truth* was the only one that featured any public criticism of Stehr's no-show. Not even Easts seemed to have a problem; the following week they named him in the starting line-up. And gave him back his captain's role.

There's no way any of that would happen today.

11

WHAT HAPPENS ON TOUR ...

There is a belief that the move to making rugby league a full-time sport gave rise to players misbehaving. The idea goes that, without a job to go to every morning, players are left with plenty of free time to fill up – usually with mischief.

While there has been a seemingly never-ending streak of players behaving badly in the modern era, that doesn't mean those from years gone by were squeaky clean. Here's a case in point – the 1947 NSW side who were kicked out of their Brisbane hotel after trashing it.

In June and July of that year, NSW and Queensland met up for four games – the first two in Sydney followed by a Brisbane double. By the time the team travelled north for the final match, NSW was unbeatable; they had a 2-1 lead in the series so the best Queensland could hope for was to tie it up. That Saturday afternoon match at the Gabba ended in a 13-all draw, ensuring the interstate title went to NSW that year. And so the celebrations began.

The bulk of the playing squad went out on the town and got hammered. When they returned to the Hotel Daniel in the wee hours of Sunday morning, they wrecked the rooms of sleeping teammates Johnny Bliss, Noel Pidding and Johnny Graves (who all chose to skip the partying). Their drunk teammates had grabbed a fire extinguisher from the hall and sprayed the sleeping trio before also tipping sand-filled ashtrays over them.

Next they tipped the beds over and snapped the legs (of the beds, not the players). Pidding, Graves and Bliss then had to walk the streets of Brisbane because they had nowhere to sleep. Meanwhile, other players were brawling with each other in the hotel corridors.

After assessing the damage later on that Sunday morning, the hotel owners placed the bill at £100 and gave the team their marching orders. Not surprisingly NSW coach Jerry O'Brien was unimpressed. 'Jerry can certainly let his head go when he likes,' an unnamed NSW player told the *Telegraph*'s George Crawford. 'We didn't mean to be offensive; we had been to a party to celebrate our successful tour and were happy. We consider the hotel manager's estimate of £100 damages is exaggerated.'

On Sunday, the team boarded their plane back to Sydney, the guilty ones with sore heads and the knowledge they would have to foot the bill for the damage caused. But only if the league could work out who was responsible; if everyone kept their mouths shut then maybe they could escape any punishment. So on the plane ride home the team – even the innocent ones – agreed to close ranks.

The league was throwing out some sizeable punishments; any player dobbed in would never go on an interstate tour, nor would they be picked for the 1948 Kangaroo tour of England

and France. Showing the media's penchant for high and mighty criticism isn't a recent development, *The Sun*'s WF Corbett gave the players a lecture in print. 'Those guilty of Sunday morning incidents appeared to feel no remorse or realise the irreparable harm that has been caused to rugby league, and the prestige of fellow players, built up so proudly in the past in Queensland.'

In the following days, NSW league secretary Keith Sharp announced the inevitable enquiry into the incident. He noted the players had already circled the wagons. 'An attempt has already been made by certain players to obscure the issue by trying to form a solid unit of the team,' Sharp said.

'This method is not expected to succeed, however, as the guiltless players realise the seriousness of the situation. Most of the players are more interested in advancing the code than shielding hooligans. When the culprits have been isolated all necessary action will be taken against them.'

While waiting for the league to reach any sort of decision, the media looked for ways to keep the story going. This included, bizarrely, blaming the league officials for the behaviour of grown men. George Crawford lambasted the league, saying they had to share the blame because they didn't provide enough entertainment for the lads. With only three training runs between their 18 July arrival and the final match on 26 July, players had plenty of time on their hands. This turned the tour into a 'pleasure jaunt', Crawford claimed.

'Night entertainment was not well organised,' Crawford wrote. 'Footballers cannot be expected to become drawing-room loungers. When entertainment is not provided, they search for it.

That is what happened last Saturday night when a number of players went off to a party.'

On 3 August, the NSWRL general committee interrogated members of the NSW squad behind closed doors for four hours. League president Harry 'Jersey' Flegg was unhappy the committee couldn't come to a decision, because the players chose not to co-operate. Flegg then threatened to name the four players involved.

The president had been in the Hotel Daniel on the night of the ruckus but had slept through it. 'I saw the damage, which was extensive, and may cost the league £100,' he said. 'A hotel porter told me the names of the players who had caused the damage. It will be a disgrace to rugby league if this incident is allowed to go unchallenged.'

In response to Flegg's outburst the league committee ordered the enquiry be re-opened. Oddly, part of that motivation was so the committee could interview Flegg about what he knew. Why the president of the league – who was staying in a room at that very hotel – hadn't come forward earlier boggles the mind. At any rate, as a result of Flegg's interview, the league cited six members of the NSW team to appear before its management committee: Frank Farrell, Noel Mulligan, Roy Hasson, Perce Pritchard, George Watt and Tom Pitman. Flegg himself would also give evidence.

In an action that smacks of a cover-up, the league was meant to send telegrams to the players informing them that their presence was required. But secretary Sharp said he had been instructed by persons unnamed not to send the telegrams.

So Flegg gave his evidence alone. Also tabled was a statement from J Polson, the hotel porter who spoke to Flegg. He confirmed the events of that weekend but, after being shown photographs of the NSW players, he declined to point the finger at any of them.

And so neither could the league, despite its president apparently knowing who they were. Instead, the league decided to sweep the whole thing under the carpet and foot the £118 damage bill. Committee chair SG Ball said the event was best forgotten. 'It is a most sorry affair and every one of the party was involved in one way or another,' he said. 'The management committee was met by a complete wall of silence. It was impossible to pin the incident to any one player.'

It seemed clear the four culprits were among the six named to appear before the committee. Curiously Ball mentioned that one player did admit his guilt but, frustratingly, didn't name him. That meant a guilty player's identity was protected while the reputations of those six others named was left under a cloud. That prompted St George committee delegate Baden Wales to ask whether those players could now be considered exonerated.

But Flegg wasn't having a bar of that. 'We all know which players were involved,' he said. 'No one will entirely be cleared of blame in the matter. If the innocent men proposed to shield the guilty, then the entire team must share the blame.

'The matter is now closed. I will not take any further part in it.'

But it didn't quite go away. The league decided not to pay the NSW players their £30 bonus. Rather than realising that punishment was fair enough, given the players chose to take the blame collectively rather than name the guilty parties, they got angry. Some considered making claims against the league for expenses incurred by having to supply their own bandages and adhesive tapes due to there being no ambulance first aid available at the Brisbane games.

Even more audacious was a request to be reimbursed for money they had spent on entertainment, because the league didn't arrange anything for them. Ultimately, saner heads prevailed with no further reports of players trying to claim a payout.

12

DRUNK

The locals who turned up at the Brisbane Exhibition Ground in late 1947 to watch the game under lights figured something was up. As a way to promote the code in the northern state, a Brisbane rep side would take on several Sydney sides. Western Suburbs had already played under lights at the venue, and St George was on their way. But the big drawcard was Canterbury, who would play the locals just days after appearing in the grand final in Sydney.

Sure, Canterbury lost that decider to Newtown 13-9 but the locals weren't too concerned about that. For them it was a chance to see how they matched up against a grand finalist from Sydney. But it shouldn't have been this easy.

At half-time the home side was up 35-2 and some of the visitors didn't really seem to be interested; there was plenty of poor passing, dropped balls and even players not paying attention to the game. As the second half went on, the 15,000-strong crowd gradually thinned out as people had had enough of the sad spectacle. Those who stayed to the final siren witnessed the home side handing out a 60-2 arse-whooping to a side who were supposed to be the second-best in the Sydney competition.

Canterbury's poor performance stunned the locals. How could this big Sydney side have let in 12 tries while only scoring a solitary penalty goal? It just didn't make sense, they thought. Something was off. And some of those Canterbury players, well, they didn't look right at all. They were staggering around, all uncoordinated, like they were … no! That couldn't be true. Surely, the players weren't … drunk?

'I am positive that three of the men of the visiting team were almost blind drunk,' attendee Allan Gordon told a journalist from *The Sun*. 'My impression was that the team had all been to a very good party before they came to the exhibition ground.' Some of the spectators pointed the finger at several in the Canterbury backline. 'The game was a farce,' said a Mr T Allen, who was also at the game. 'One of the backs was so drunk that he could not take a ball.'

The spectacle was so unimpressive that an Ipswich side cancelled a planned match with Canterbury. 'After hearing reports of representatives of this league who saw the exhibition given by the visitors in Brisbane,' Ipswich League president E Patrick said, 'we decided that no good purpose would be served by staging the game.'

After that Monday night debacle, club secretary Barney Russell carpeted the side back at the team hotel before the Canterbury team flew home in disgrace on Wednesday. Some in the team were obviously unhappy with the performance of their teammates, freely leaking to the media that they knew as many as four players were drunk on the field. There was also talk of players being thrown under cold showers before the match in a forlorn effort to sober them up.

Not surprisingly, a press contingent was waiting at Mascot for their plane to land. Some played a straight bat to the allegations, such as forward Ken Charlton, who said there was no truth to the claims. Others, like lock Len Holmes claimed the heavy loss was because many of his teammates were not used to playing under lights.

Instead of keeping his mouth shut, Holmes then cracked open the door to reality. 'Some of the players had a few drinks during the afternoon but none was under the influence of liquor,' he foolishly said. 'The boys were around Brisbane all day, and we met many friends. It is natural to have a couple of drinks, but the drinking finished long before the match started.'

The bigwigs in the Sydney league took the allegation very seriously, going so far as raising the spectre of lifetime bans from the game. 'This is the first time in the history of rugby league that we have had to deal with anything of this nature,' said NSWRL president Harry Flegg. 'It is alleged that certain players were drunk, and that is detrimental to the game. The league never disqualifies players for life, but has often outed men for the pleasure of the committee, which means they never play again.'

One person who had had enough was Canterbury coach Ross McKinnon. Disgusted by the shenanigans of some in his team, McKinnon threw in the towel. 'I had practically made up my mind to resign before the Brisbane episode,' he said, 'but any faint chance of my continuing as coach has been eliminated by the behaviour of the team up north.

'I have business friends who won't appreciate my association with a team of footballers who have let down their club, their supporters and their officials.'

Canterbury co-manager Mr H Culbert admitted, in hindsight, the club's decision to pay each player a £5 bonus on the morning of the game may not have been the wisest idea – it seems a number of players plonked that money down on a bar or spent it in a bottle shop. That undoubtedly contributed to the problem, as did the fact the players had a whole day to fill before kick-off at 7.30 pm. As Holmes said, players went out and had a few drinks with mates in the morning. Then the players met up for lunch before they headed to the ground at 2 pm and were left to their own devices until 5.30 pm. To kill time, the players started a two-up school, which no doubt involved more boozing.

The players who were accused of taking the field drunk were fullback Dick Johnson and hooker Bob Baxter (while a league report stated four players had been smashed, curiously only Johnson and Baxter were named).

Johnson, who was taken off the field at half-time, had an inventive explanation as to why he may have seemed drunk when he really wasn't – malaria.

'At half-time I found it was impossible for me to continue playing and I went to hospital to seek treatment,' Johnson said. 'I had four years in the army and anybody who has suffered from malaria will know that I was suffering from the symptoms of the "wog" and not drink.'

However, in another instance of someone not knowing when to shut up, Johnson explained he'd had three whiskies on the morning of the match – which he claimed was an effective way to treat a flare-up of malaria. Then, in the afternoon he attended an RAAF reunion and had at least four beers. So, even though he was drinking in the morning and the afternoon, it was the malaria, and not the drink – got it?

In a club investigation all four players were reprimanded, but officials only mentioned Johnson and Baxter at a NSWRL inquiry. They may have been the two players declared 'really drunk' by co-manager Culbert in the league inquiry.

Two further players were cited but not punished – Holmes and half Jim Collins. Holmes' offence was relatively minor; he turned up in the hotel dining room inappropriately dressed. Collins was in hot water for chundering in the rooftop garden at the team hotel (though he did then clean it up himself). In an echo of his teammate's words, Collins insisted he was ill, not drunk. His club bought that story.

Club secretary Russell chose to ignore the way the wind was blowing and launched into a long and poorly thought-out defence of his players.

He claimed the 60-2 thumping was not actually out of the ordinary at all. 'We did not have players of sufficient ability to win against the team we played,' he said of his team that made the grand final. 'You can never do better than you are capable of doing. There might be a tendency to take credit away from a good team of footballers.'

Then he doubled down, suggesting that it was ridiculous that the Brisbane side could only score 60 points 'against a team that was supposed to have been in a drunken orgy'. As arguments go, it was pretty flimsy, but worse was to come. Without stating whether it was Johnson or Baxter, Russell said he had gambled with the player during that two-up game – and he would never have done that had the player been sloshed. 'I had an interest in the bank with one of the players who is charged,' he said. 'Do you think I would have trusted him with my money if he had been drunk?'

The league didn't have access to the rose-coloured glasses Russell was wearing and fined the club £200 and suspended the pair until 31 July 1948 – meaning they would miss the first 14 games of the 18-game season.

Johnson was not happy with the suspension and planned to take the league to court 'to show that I was suffering from malaria at the time, and was not drunk.'

'I am 31 and have held a good name in rugby league for many years but I am not going out of the game with this stigma hanging over me,' he said. 'I want to go out of the game with flying colours and, if I retired now, the public would consider me guilty.'

Baxter admitted he had 'a couple of beers' in the morning but was a cleanskin after lunch. 'Football is my life and if I am suspended on a charge of which I am not guilty, it may ruin my career,' he said.

Johnson appeared not to have gone through with his legal threat, though the club decided to appeal the pair's suspension in March before the start of the 1948 season. 'We are confident that something can be done about the ban,' Russell said. That confidence was misplaced – by a vote of 21-11 the league refused to lift the suspension.

Johnson returned to the field for the Round 11 match against Western Suburbs and played for five games before being left out for the last three rounds. That year Canterbury finished in fifth, five points out of the top four.

As for the reserve-grader Baxter, after playing three first-grade matches in 1947, he didn't return to the top league until 1950, playing six games over the following two seasons. Maybe things could have worked out better for him without that black mark against his name.

THE WOMAN TWICE RANG THE POLICE SAYING LULHAM HAD BEEN POISONED BUT WOULD NOT GIVE HER NAME.

13

MURDER AND THE MOTHER-IN-LAW

In Round 12 of the 1953 season, Balmain's Bobby Lulham had a great game. The winger scored all of his team's 13 points in their win over Manly at Brookvale Oval. A week later they rolled St George 26-12, with Lulham – who had played for Australia and was part of the NSW team during that infamous 1947 trip to Brisbane – scoring 17 of his team's points.

But he had a shocker in the next game against Canterbury. He didn't score a point in the 14-7 loss, and was slow across the field, regularly getting smashed by opponents before he could pass the ball. Lulham's performance was so poor he was hooted by the Leichhardt Oval crowd.

He knew he wasn't right, complaining of a heavy feeling in his legs before the game. But he took the field anyway, not wanting to let down his teammates. On Monday, 20 July – two days after the game – he went to his job as a truck driver but collapsed and went home sick. Two days later he would discover the reason why – and it would create quite a scandal, easily on par with anything the modern-day footballer can come up with.

Lulham was suffering the effects of thallium poisoning. Marketed as rat poison Thall-rat and bought by many households, thallium was involved in a spate of poisonings in Sydney in the late 1940s and early 1950s. Between March 1952 and May 1953, there were 46 reported cases of poisoning, many of which were attempts to murder a person. Indeed of those 46 cases, 10 ended in death.

On the Tuesday night, Lulham was admitted to the Royal Prince Alfred Hospital with symptoms of thallium poisoning – limb numbness and hair falling out. The penny had dropped when NSWRL medical officer Dr Greenberg got a call on Monday from a woman saying her husband had put rat poison in Luhlam's beer while he was drinking at the pub.

The doctor then called the club, who told him that Lulham was suffering from the flu. So Greenberg put it out of his mind until the next day when he discovered Lulham was seriously ill and called the police. On Wednesday, the woman twice rang the police saying Lulham had been poisoned but would not give her name.

The Balmain winger himself was at a loss to help police track down his poisoner. 'I haven't an enemy in the world that I know of,' he said. 'I just haven't a clue. It has me beaten. I have thought and thought about it night and day, but have no idea who could have done it.'

His father-in-law Alf Monty, however, had a theory – it had been done in the dressing rooms after a game. 'Anybody can walk into the players' dressing room at suburban grounds,' he said. 'It is not uncommon for players to be handed a glass of beer by enthusiastic fans and it would be possible for a spectator

– one who perhaps lost money on the game – to slap him on the back and say, "You played a great game. Here, have a beer".'

A few weeks later, on 6 August, police made a surprising arrest – Luhlam's 45-year-old mother-in-law Veronica Monty. The police charged her with the attempted murder of Lulham, alleging she secretly gave him the thallium some time in early July. After being bailed out of jail, two days later Monty herself was in hospital, also suffering from thallium poisoning.

She would end up in the same hospital as Lulham, who was eventually discharged on 19 August. Several weeks later he took part in Monty's committal hearing to see if there was enough evidence to send her to trial. Lulham must have been dreading that moment, knowing what was likely to come out. If the people of Sydney thought the attempted poisoning of a rugby league player was a great story, it was about to get a whole lot juicier.

During interviews with Monty, police claimed she told them she had been intimate with Lulham on several occasions while living in the house with him and his wife Judith (Monty was separated from husband Alf). She also said she suspected Lulham of playing around, claiming she had found lipstick and make-up on his shirt. Despite that, when asked whether she was in love with her 26-year-old son-in-law, police said she told them 'I like him very much'.

Regarding the attempted murder of Lulham, Monty said the thallium was intended for her. Feeling depressed she made herself a hot milk drink, mixing in some thallium. When Judith and Bobby asked if she could make them one each she did so.

She claimed she got the glasses mixed up and gave Bobby the one with the poison.

Police also alleged Monty was the woman who had called several times claiming to know who poisoned him. She later said the calls were made as a way to ensure Lulham got the medical help he needed.

The court heard that one of the times Monty and Lulham had been intimate was while they sat on the lounge listening to the second Ashes cricket Test. She had raised concerns about Judith's happiness in the marriage and Lulham, believing there was nothing wrong, suggested he would go and wake up his wife and ask her.

Monty insisted he shouldn't do that, instead he should stay on the lounge with her. Soon thereafter, there was some passionate kissing. 'I think we both stretched out on the lounge and got comfortable,' Lulham said. 'After several kisses we became a little familiar with one another. There was no intercourse or anything like that.' Indeed, while police alleged Monty admitted intercourse had indeed taken place, both of them would later insist they never went all the way.

The pair also got together while Judith was away at Mass on a Sunday morning and again on that Monday when Lulham came home sick from work. Lulham told the court Monty had entered his bedroom and sat on his bed. She then removed her underwear, lay down beside him and 'a similar incident occurred' is how a no-doubt embarrassed Lulham phrased it.

Despite the marital mess, Lulham maintained that Monty would never have tried to murder him, noting that she prepared the meals at home and so would have had ample opportunities to poison him if she wanted to.

The judge decided there was enough evidence to send Monty's case to trial. While waiting for the December trial, Monty and her daughter would live at the home in Ryde, while Lulham headed to the North Coast.

The trial captured the attention of Sydney with a long line of women queuing up at the courtroom doors armed with a packed lunch waiting to be let in each morning. The key players all had to parade their domestic secrets in public again, Lulham adding the detail that things never went further than a 'petting party' despite the fact that clothing was removed or rearranged. It was also revealed that he had a pet name for Monty – 'Tops' – and that he kissed her every day when he left for work and when he arrived back home.

Facing two charges – attempted murder and maliciously administering a poison – Monty pleaded not guilty to both. On the night in question, she said she had meant to take the poison herself and spent some time waiting for the results but to no avail.

'But I was in for a rude awakening because what seemed like an apparently simple illness on Bobby's part developed, and the stark horror of it struck me – that Bobby must have got what I intended for myself.' At that point she couldn't come clean because people 'would have thought the worst of me' for trying to commit suicide. So she instead made a number of phone calls saying Lulham was poisoned to make sure he got the medical attention he needed.

Monty escaped a jail sentence, being found not guilty on both charges. She celebrated the verdict with friends at Como; estranged husband Alf and daughter Judith were also there. Lest those celebrations suggest there was some level of forgiveness of Veronica, double divorces were on their way.

A week later, Alf made their separation permanent, while Judith decided to end her marriage to the man she had been with since she was 15. In granting both divorces, Justice Dovey decided not to go through the 'nauseating details of the disgusting incidents' of the affair.

'I am satisfied that Lulham did not initiate the intimacies on any occasion,' he said. 'I am convinced he was seduced into participation in what has been quite properly described as scandalous conduct, and has been seduced into that position by the woman charged.

'She may be properly criticised for breaking the marriage, which showed such promise, of having all that could be desired.'

Monty decided to sell her story to the Sydney *Truth*. While the front page of the 13 December issue carried the news of the double divorce, Veronica Mabel Monty told her story in a two-page spread, under the headline 'I betrayed my own daughter'. Apparently having not had her fill of airing dirty laundry in public, Monty kept going.

'My real heartache is for my daughter,' she wrote. 'No one will know the agonies I have suffered in the knowledge that it was I who wrecked her married happiness. I feel I must go away where people don't know me and give Judy a chance to forget the wrongs she has suffered.'

Those who were hoping for more salacious details of what she and Bobby got up to would be disappointed. There was nothing new in her story and she only mentioned the night on the lounge listening to the cricket. She claimed 'some kind of dreadful loneliness drove me into the arms of my son-in-law. There is no doubt I loved him deeply. But I must have been mad to show it.'

Regarding the purchase of thallium, she said she had no need for it and was not thinking clearly when she bought it. 'My mind was in torment and I seemed to be losing control. I began to develop suicidal tendencies.'

Those tendencies didn't go away once the court case was over. In April 1955, Monty was working as a barmaid at the Union Hotel in North Sydney under the alias of Vera Morgan. On 17 April, after having a few glasses of brandy, Veronica shot herself with her employer's pistol in a bedroom of the hotel. Despite all that had happened, Judith broke down when police told her that her mother was dead.

THE TEAM WAS SCREWED – LAWLER HAD BACKED THE OTHER SIDE.

14

BEATING THE REF

In 1963 beaten grand finalists Western Suburbs were sure they had a reason to hate referee Darcy Lawler. The referee who had taken charge of more than 300 matches and seven grand finals is now mainly remembered for claims he had a punt on the Dragons to win in the '63 decider – a game for which he was out in the middle.

Wests prop Jack Gibson (yes, that Jack Gibson) had a foot in the shady side of Sydney having worked as a bouncer in various nightclubs. Whispers had found their way to his ear that Lawler had had a big plunge on the Dragons – a whopping £600. On match day, with the rain pouring down turning the SCG into a mud bath, Gibson sat down next to captain Noel Kelly in the sheds before the game and told him the team was screwed – Lawler had backed the other side. There was no way Wests, the team that was the only one to beat the Dragons that season (three times – twice in the regular season and again in the major semi-final) was going to come away with the chocolates on grand final day.

'It was the biggest disappointment of my career,' Kelly said years later. 'Wests should have won that grand final. We were the better side of the day. We were never going to win that game. We knew before we ran out onto the field we were going to be up against it. How do you think it felt sitting there in the dressing room before the grand final, knowing you were not going to be allowed to win it?'

After this match, the iconic 'Gladiators' photo of Arthur Summons and Norm Provan embracing was taken. It's an image immortalised in the NRL's grand final trophy, which is a tad amusing given that, at the time the photo was being taken, Summons was giving Provan a gobful about how the ref helped the Dragons win.

The prime piece of evidence Wests players point to as proof Lawler wasn't playing it straight was Dragons winger Johnny King's try. At the back end of the second half, with the score 5-3 in the Dragons favour and Wests looking like they were coming back, King started on a run down the wing.

Despite the heavy going on the muddy turf, he managed to break the tackle of a Wests defender before slipping as he got to cover defender Don Parish. The Wests fullback also slipped over and then had his efforts to grab King again thwarted when Gibson came over the top and knocked Parish back to the ground.

King then got up and continued running, eventually scoring a try in the corner that took the Dragons out to a five-point lead. Numerous Wests players contend that King was held in the tackle, though footage of the incident shows the arm carrying the ball never hits the turf. They have also insisted Lawler called 'held', which caused Wests players to relax.

'I swear to this day I heard Lawler yell "play it" when Parish put King down,' Summons said. 'So did others, and we momentarily relaxed.'

But the footage shows the Wests' cover defence didn't relax but continued to head towards the sideline to cut off King, even after they claim the Dragons winger was called to play the ball. To a modern-day viewer, it looks like King was perfectly entitled to get up and continue running; certainly, his forward momentum was never checked.

If Lawler had bet on St George and needed them to win so he didn't lose £600, he did make some on-field decisions that definitely weren't in his best interests. When the sides came back onto the field after half-time, the score was 5-0 to the Dragons. Twenty minutes later, Lawler made a decision that he didn't have to make, a decision that put his wad of cash in serious jeopardy – he awarded a try to Wests. A try right next to the posts.

Summons kicked the ball forward, forcing fullback Graeme Langlands to scurry across the field to gather it in. He got up to play the ball but Summons at marker was all over him. Footage shows Summons leaning on Langlands' back as he plays the ball, and they both fall over.

That made things hard for dummy half King, who misjudged the roll of the ball, and Wests centre Bob McGuinness stepped in to toe the ball forward over the try line and he and Gil MacDougall bustled each other to see who would score – the latter getting there first. Lawler wasted no time in awarding the try, which with a kick to come from adjacent to the posts, could level up the game. But Parish missed a simple conversion, slipping over in the process.

If Lawler was looking for a reason not to award the try and save his cash, then he just needed to ping Summons for interfering with the play-the-ball. It would be a penalty people would struggle to argue with, and would totally be in keeping with what you'd expect of a referee with a heavy wager on the Dragons. And yet he acted against his own best interests – if he indeed had cash on the Dragons, that is.

The 1963 grand final wasn't the first time Lawler had made someone angry. Early in his career, there were several times a spectator tried to punch him – and two of them after the same game.

The first was after a 1951 match between Newtown and Souths. Lawler awarded the match-winning try to Souths' Bryan Orrock, beating Newtown 23-17. That and being on the wrong end of a 25-12 penalty count had Newtown fans hot under the collar. They didn't pay attention to their own kicker's abysmal performance, landing just one of nine attempts. Nope, it had to be the ref's fault.

Lawler was jeered as he walked off Pratten Park, with at least three men trying to lay some fives on him. One got close enough to grab Lawler, only to be pushed away by a touch judge.

The mood was fiery in the Newtown sheds, which was no good for Lawler, who had to walk through them to get to his own changing rooms. On his way through, he insisted he was abused by a supporter in a Newtown blazer and demanded the club identify him – which they never did.

Newtown captain Frank Farrell was not impressed with Lawler either, telling anyone who would listen 'we were robbed!' A journalist in the Newtown sheds reported on Farrell's outburst, though chose to leave out all the 'purple expletives'.

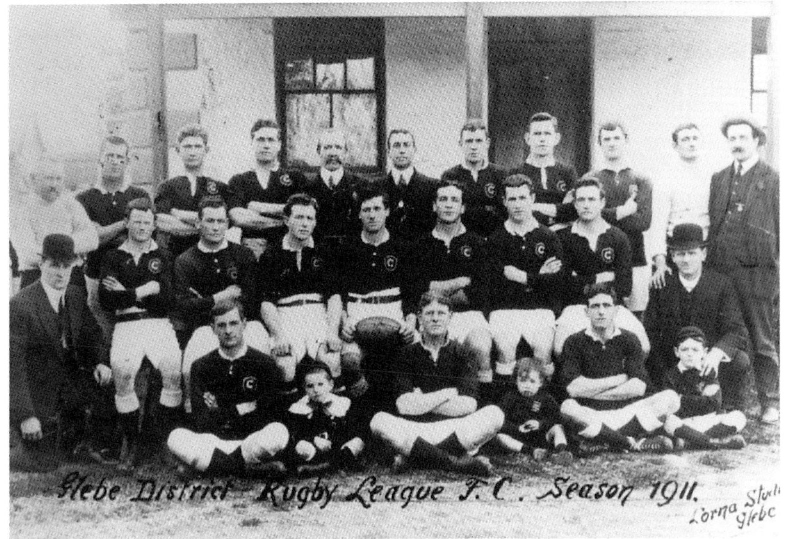

ABOVE The Glebe first grade team in 1911. Six years later the club had a stoush with the league that saw the whole top grade side suspended.

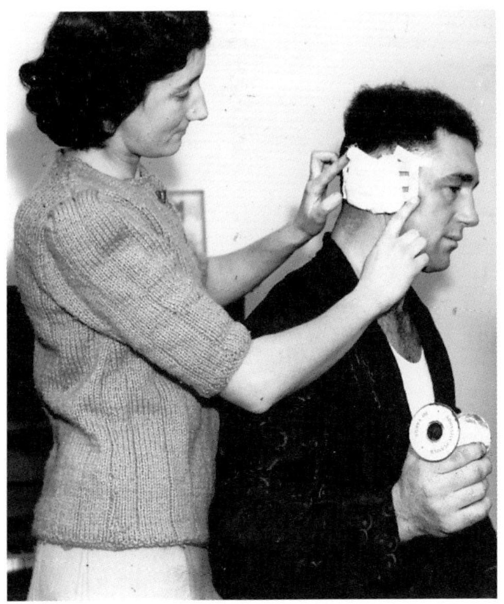

LEFT St George prop forward Bill McRitchie's wife takes care of a dressing following an infamous ear biting incident in a 1945 match against Newtown.

RIGHT Newtown captain Frank 'Bumper' Farrell was identified by McRitchie – and others – as the ear biter, though he insisted he couldn't have done it because his false teeth were in the dressing sheds at the time.

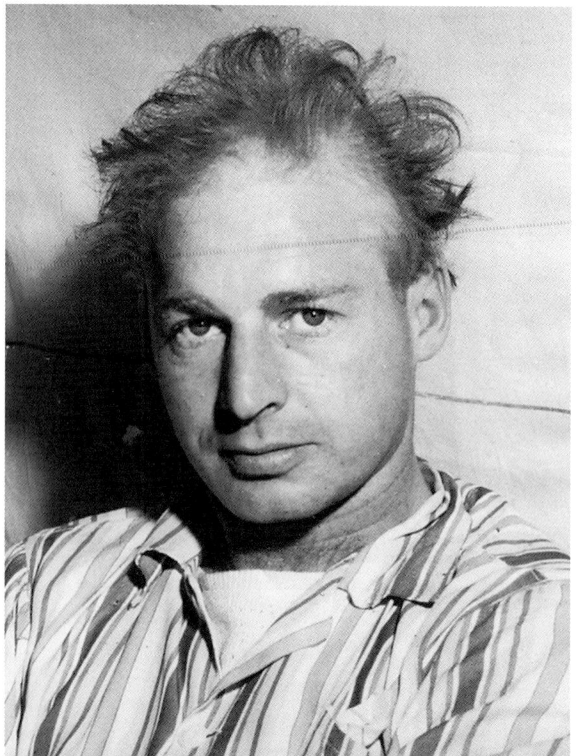

ABOVE Balmain winger Bobby Lulham dives over the line to score against Newtown at the Sydney Cricket Ground.

LEFT Lulham in hospital after doctors realised he'd been a victim of thallium poisoning.

LEFT Bobby Lulham outside court during the trial of his mother-in-law Veronica Monty over his poisoning. The trial drew plenty of attention due to extra-marital high-jinks between Lulham and his mother-in-law.

BELOW Judith Lulham with her mother entering the courthouse. The daughter supported her mother during the trial, though it was short-lived.

Crowd on roof of outer stand

ABOVE The novelty of having the American All-Stars in town for a rugby league tour drew a crowd of 65,453 to the Sydney Cricket Ground to watch their first game.

BELOW The Americans warmed up before matches. The then accepted wisdom in league circles was this was a waste of time and only wore out a team before the match.

ABOVE Western Suburbs forward Jack Gibson is taken to the SCG turf by St George defenders in the 1963 grand final. Gibson was adamant referee Darcy Lawler had backed the Dragons to win.

LEFT Controversial referee Darcy Lawler prior to running out for the 1963 grand final. Earlier in his career some of his decisions led to spectators trying to punch him as he left the field.

ABOVE Dennis Tutty arriving at the High Court with his lawyer David McKenzie to hear the ruling on the league's transfer rule. He won the case, which made it easier for every player from that point on to switch clubs.

LEFT St George captain Graeme Langlands leaves the field wearing his infamous white boots in the 1975 grand final flogging at the hands of the Roosters.

RIGHT Eastern Suburbs captain Arthur Beetson sporting a jersey emblazoned with its new sponsor. In 1976, the Roosters were the first club to sign up a jersey sponsor.

LEFT American import Manfred Moore prepares to hurl a football gridiron-style over the grandstand at Henson Park in 1977.

BELOW The Super Bowl winner Moore found league harder than he expected, saying that 'every hit hurts'.

'I tackled Orrock and had hold of the ball, which was six inches away from the line,' Farrell said. 'I told the referee to take a look for himself, but the referee said nothing, he simply awarded a try.'

Lawler must have heard Farrell's spray because it was mentioned in his match report. That led to the league suspending the Newtown captain for misconduct, ordering he sit on the sidelines for one match.

Farrell, a Sydney policeman, said he would appeal the decision even though he would have served the one-match ban before the appeal was heard. 'I resent the fact that Lawler had two touch judges to back him up last night yet I was not invited to bring anyone with me,' Farrell said. 'I was invited to attend the inquiry and merely considered it an investigation. Unfortunately there can be no appeal before next Monday night so I will have to miss Saturday's match with Manly. However I intend to have my name cleared.' But his efforts were to no avail with the league choosing not to re-hear the case and to let the penalty stand.

In April of the following season, things got worse for Lawler – he was punched three times by spectators in a matter of two weeks. Two of them after the same match.

The first bunch of fives he copped came in a Round 4 match between Balmain and Souths at Leichhardt Oval. A few minutes before full time, Lawler awarded a try to Souths' Les Cowie, which won the game – much to the displeasure of the home-town crowd. Balmain supporter John Henry Seymour saw red and jumped the fence and king-hit the ref as he stood on the spot the try was scored.

Seymour threw two 'rabbit killer' punches, knocking Lawler to the ground and then jumped back into the crowd.

Newspaper reports said Seymour was chased by up to 200 people as he ran from the oval. Making it outside the ground, he was spotted by two police officers who chased him for a mile before arresting him at a hotel.

A second man punched Lawler as he left the field but managed to escape. Other spectators were too busy throwing garbage at Lawler to give chase. Cowie too had a punch thrown at him as he left the field.

Seymour appeared in court a day later, charged with punching Lawler. 'It was in the heat of the moment,' he told the court. 'I was carried away when the crowd started booing and howling down the referee.' The magistrate fined him £5 and said 'an action like this could have caused a riot'.

Two weeks later at the Sydney Sports Ground, a match between Souths and Newtown saw a whole load of punches thrown – one of them in Lawler's direction. Four players – two from each side – were sent off for fighting, while a fifth was marched for backchatting Lawler. 'Bryan Orrock [Souths] and John Lightfoot [Newtown] fought on the ground 60 yards from play,' the *Telegraph* reported of the second-half fisticuffs. 'They went off after linesman T Grew had reported the scuffle to Lawler. Two scrums later the two packs fought furiously in a free-for-all. A South Sydney forward was felled from behind. International Bernie Purcell and Newtown lock Don Solah stood in the open and punched each other.'

As Purcell and Solah left the field, the Newtown lock was set upon by spectators, one of whom laid a punch on him. A woman got involved too, swinging her umbrella at Solah. 'Next thing, punches were coming at me from all angles,' Solah said, 'and I was bailed up against a wall copping everything, including the umbrella.'

Injured teammate Jack Troy stepped in to offer assistance, punching a few spectators in the process. After that, the last five minutes of the game was 'more fight than football,' according to the *Telegraph*.

At full time, Lawler left the field and had a spectator take a swing at him and then have a go at a touch judge. Police were called to stand guard outside the referee's dressing room. Newtown captain Farrell used the incident to have a dig at Lawler, claiming he lost control of the match and that at least one Newtown player was sent off unnecessarily. Newtown official Jack Kessey said he was going to complain about Lawler to the league because, as is often the case with a brawl, officials tend to blame the ref rather than their own players.

At the judiciary, Newtown's Vic Carter was suspended for two weeks for backchatting, while Purcell and Solah each got a one-week stint on the sidelines. Orrock and Lightfoot escaped with severe cautions. Lawler didn't escape unscathed; after being assaulted several times in a few weeks, the league decided to drop him to reserve grade.

The news of the brawl – and the recent rough treatment of Lawler – made it all the way to Queensland, where Brisbane's

The Sunday Mail said the source of the recent violence was people gambling on games.

'Whenever, for appearance's sake, questions have been asked, club officials have denied any knowledge of or connection with betting, players have chorused shocked protests, and authorities have pointed out how difficult it would be to police all grounds,' the paper's 'Insider' columnist stated.

'Betting goes on though, in a more organised way than ever, and it wouldn't take any investigating committee long to gather unpleasant evidence if it wanted to.

'The woman who recently wielded an umbrella with some effect and the spectators who, on two different Saturdays, attacked referee Darcy Lawler, probably were only reacting to a sharp pain in the pocket, much as disgruntled punters do.'

15

AMERICAN ALL-STARS

Blowout scorelines, favourable referee decisions, teams letting their opponent score, officials being snubbed, a case of polio, crowds booing a future Immortal, a promoter looking to make 'a fast dollar' and concerns the touring team might not even make it to Australia in the first place – welcome to the 1953 American All-Stars tour.

The tour was the brainchild of American promoter/player Mike Dimitro, who said he had become familiar with league while stationed in Australia during World War II. After teeing up the tour, he set about recruiting players – most of whom were students from Stanford, the University of Southern California and UCLA. Many had played American football (though some were wrestlers), but rugby league would be a completely new experience for all.

Even before the first game, there were concerns about the tour taking place. Newspaper reports in April flagged concern that the airline the team was using had cancelled their flights due to lack of payment. Dimitro told the league all was good – they had just changed to a different carrier. Perhaps realising how skint the promoter was – and how foolish the league might look – it guaranteed the team's return airfares at the end of the tour.

Before he even arrived, *The Sun* newspaper gave Dimitro both barrels claiming he was 'motivated by the chance of making a fast dollar.'

'Dimitro, who has Australian rugby league officials dangling like puppets,' the paper said, 'is a shoestring promoter, a man of straw and a liar when it suits him to be.'

The paper said a US staff member had interviewed Dimitro and was invited to attend training at USC. When the journalist arrived on the appointed day, there was no sign of the players or Dimitro. The story also noted Dimitro said All-American gridiron star Bob Waterfield was on the team and would be bringing his wife, actress Jane Russell, to Australia. Both very quickly denied they were heading down under.

If the league read the story it would certainly have raised a few concerns. The last lines of the story wouldn't have sat well with them at all. 'This Flegg's Follies tour is the most haphazard sporting venture of all time. It could make rugby league look silly and, what is infinitely more serious, make Australia look silly.'

So the league likely breathed a sigh of relief when the team's plane touched down in Sydney on 18 May. Dimitro's squad numbered 20 players and they would play 19 games in NSW and Queensland before heading to New Zealand for another eight matches.

There were barely two weeks before their first match, against Monaro-Southern Division in Canberra which meant their appointed coach Norm 'Latchem' Robinson (who would go on to coach the Australian side) had his work cut out for him.

Dimitro didn't quite see it that way, however. 'We are here to learn the finer points of the game and will learn enough within the next eight days to put up a good showing for our first match,' he said.

'When I say we do not expect difficulty in transferring to the league code it is because there is not much difference as far as basic essentials of football are concerned. Gridiron football has everything that rugby league has in handling, passing, tackling, running with the ball and kicking for the line and goal.'

He also talked up plans to establish an organisation in the US to control and promote rugby league, and put a playing tour of the US on the table.

The team played a few warm-up matches, including a touch football game with South Sydney, where they impressed watching journalists. 'The American scrummaging will be tightened in the next few days,' the *Telegraph* reported. 'The Americans are good handlers and all have ball sense. At present their positional play is astray, but they have the newest thing in league – the 40-yard one-hand pass.' Ah yes, you just knew the one-handed spiral would make an appearance.

The one warm-up match where scores were kept was against a team from the Royal Australian Engineers Unit at Casula army base. Oddly, several newspaper reports neglect to include the final score which is suggestive of them leaving before it was over. For the record the Americans won 41-10, though reporters who stayed to the end said the referee gave the newcomers an awful lot of latitude.

A few day later at Manuka Oval in Canberra, the visitors provided a shock by beating Monaro-Southern Division 34-25. According to The *Canberra Times*, more than 6000 people – 'the largest crowd to attend any football match in Canberra' – turned up to watch the Americans in their long-sleeved royal blue jerseys and three-quarter length pants decorated in red, white and blue.

They saw the All-Stars come back from a 20-8 half-time deficit. Country Rugby League secretary DF Locke said the home team didn't take it easy on the visitors either. The spiral pass made an appearance too, via the arm of centre Gary Kerkorian. 'Almost every time Kerkorian raised his arm to spiral the ball to a waiting player,' wrote EE Christensen, 'the crowd gasped in anticipation, even though the manoeuvre sometimes lost ground.' Or set up the receiver to be smashed by the defence rushing up on him while he waited, flatfooted, for the ball to arrive.

If the All-Stars thought this league caper was pretty easy to master, they got a reality check three days later at the SCG. A Sydney team made up of the likes of Clive Churchill, Noel Pidding and Ken Kearney thumped them 52-25. But it was more about the spectacle than the scoreline; the match was so popular that police had to close the gates before kick-off. Some bright sparks took advantage of a dog show at the showground next door, buying themselves a ticket and then watching the game from the outside stairwells and roof of the neighbouring grandstand.

The spectators got to see the amusing sight of the Americans warming up before the match; it was accepted wisdom in Australia that such activities were unnecessary and just wore you out before the match. They marvelled at Kerkorian's eight-from-eight goal kicking effort, where he placed the ball upright, took two steps back and roosted it between the posts.

The younger – and female – section of the crowd were also interested in what might happen after the match. For as long as an hour after the game, a horde of teenage girls swirled outside the members' stand entrance, waiting for the visitors to appear. While many wanted just an autograph, some were after something more. Especially in the case of one teen wearing a bright red zippered sweater, with the zipper clip carrying the tag 'Give me a Yank'.

As far as the sport was concerned, the next game was a joke – NSW won 62-41 after leading 31-20 at half-time. 'During the second half NSW players often stood aside and allowed the Americans to score,' the *Telegraph*'s George Crawford reported. 'NSW hooker Ken Kearney, in a generous mood, often tapped the ball through the scrums to the Americans.

'NSW winger Noel Pidding, who scored two tries, crossed the line on two other occasions, but presented the ball to teammates instead of scoring himself.'

The blowouts didn't worry NSW Board of Control Secretary Harold Matthews, who said the tour would not be cut short to avoid further embarrassing scorelines. However he refused to comment on the 62-41 debacle.

Dimitro had no such qualms, stating part of the problem was the high number of his team playing injured. He had underestimated the amount of players needed for a 19-match Australian tour with short turnarounds between matches; players were dropping like flies. He also insisted that, with a bit more time, his team would close the gap with the local rep teams.

'We've been here a fortnight,' he said. 'Six weeks hence I figured my boys could beat Australia. And I'm not kidding.'

But at this point, they couldn't beat their next two opponents in Combined Country or Western Division. The former match was played in Wollongong, where the All-Stars snubbed the city by not attending a dinner and mayoral reception organised in their honour.

'Nobody told me about this reception,' Dimitro protested. 'We appreciate Australian hospitality and we would be the last in the world to offend anyone.' Which didn't explain why a similar thing occurred in Canberra after the first tour match, where just three American players turned up to the special reception. Nor would it explain the other times players dodged events held in their honour.

On the field, the Americans got back into the winners' column by defeating a Newcastle rep side 19-10. The home side was without their five state representatives and media reports stated the refereeing was lenient towards the Americans. 'The Americans had instructions to stand up on the Newcastle team in the second half,' *The Sun* reported, 'and referee Aub Oxford often allowed them to be glaringly off-side in play-the-ball and scrum movements.'

After another loss – to a Northern NSW team at Coffs Harbour – the Americans headed to Queensland for nine matches. It was either an indication of the different levels of teams in NSW compared to Queensland, or a measure that the

US team was actually improving, but the scorelines north of the border were much tighter.

While they only won a solitary match (16-15 against Ipswich), the biggest defeat was 38-17 against North Queensland and they drew with Wide Bay and Far North Queensland. Most surprising was a 39-36 loss to the Queensland state side, where the visitors showed they had learned enough about the game to criticise the referee's decisions.

Dimitro felt one try was awarded after a shepherd and another from a forward pass. 'The Americans received no leniency from referee Ballard,' George Crawford noted. 'He awarded them only seven penalties to Queensland's five – a vast difference in the margin the Americans had received from more lenient NSW referees.'

The All-Stars sole Queensland win came in what 'was one of the dirtiest and wildest in Queensland for years'. Due to injuries, the visitors had to use two Brisbane rugby players to fill out the side in a game where the second half was full of punches and kicks. 'Once the American Albans lost his temper and kicked Ipswich forward Rashleigh after a tackle,' The *Telegraph* reported. 'The incident happened in front of a linesman and Albans should have been sent off. Once, Albans tried to attack the referee. American manager Mike Dimitro and winger Bob Buckley pulled Albans to the ground.

'Forwards also used their fists during the second half. At one stage there were groups of players exchanging punches.'

All-Star Jack Bonetti got some very bad news while in a Townsville hospital suffering a slipped disc. Doctors eventually discovered he had contracted polio. 'I thought, "why me?"

I didn't smoke or drink and had no affairs and yet it was me who came down with polio,' he later said.

The league later donated £50 to help Bonetti and South Sydney chipped in £20. Six seats from a DC3 had to be removed to create a separate compartment for Bonetti to fly back to Sydney before eventually flying home.

The tour itself was also in trouble. There were reports some American players were fed up and wanted it to finish as soon as possible, and rumours it would be cut short started to be bandied about. Board secretary Matthews denied that any such plan was being considered.

There was also a difference of opinion on just how profitable the tour had been (which, if everyone is being honest, was the main driver of the tour). Matthews talked up the success of the tour, claiming most Queensland matches raked in more than £1000 each. But Dimitro said he was still around £7000 short of breaking even – with just two more matches left to recoup that.

'I have paid each of the players £6 a week during his stay here,' Dimitro said. 'Only 60 per cent of the gates has not helped us.

'I understand that Frenchmen were given 65 per cent of the gates during their tour. The anticipated expenses of about £20,000 include our fares back to America, via New Zealand. If we do not pick up £7000 in the two games in Sydney, I expect to gain a profit during the tour of New Zealand.

'Added to that we are to play two gridiron games in Honolulu on our way back to the United States. This will boost our finances.'

Also, hopes of the tour being a fillip for the establishment of the game in the United States started to fade by the end.

None of the team interviewed by the media 'painted rosy pictures of league's future in America', reported *The Courier-Mail.* At best, they felt there could only be a short season of January to March – sandwiched in between the end of the gridiron season and the start of baseball.

Matthews' claim that the tour would not be curtailed ended up to be false. Following a 27-18 loss to NSW (who had flogged the visitors earlier in the tour) Matthews cancelled the last game because the Americans had run out of healthy players to put on the field.

That final match against NSW was notable because it saw Jack Gibson make his state debut. It also saw the local crowd boo none other than Clive Churchill for his performance.

'In the farcical first half,' wrote *The Sun*'s Geoff Allen, 'Churchill's poor attempts at tackles had let the Americans in for two tries, by Davies and Albans. Churchill was booed when he failed to get near Davies, who had dashed 40 yards to score. Later, the crowd just laughed when the NSW captain made a late dive that failed by two feet to stop Albans going over for a try.'

The Americans would leave for New Zealand under a cloud. Dimitro was unhappy to be £4500 out of pocket on the tour, while further stories emerged of the team failing to turn up for events held in their honour. That happened after a match at Gundagai and St George's Baden Wells told the NSWRL the club had arranged a function for the team and even sent five cars over to pick them up – only to find the players still asleep in bed. It cast into doubt any plans the league may have had for a formal farewell function.

Before he could escape, a Sydney car hire firm took Dimitro to court over an unpaid bill of £44. He told the court he had written out a cheque for the amount and was surprised to be told he may be held by the court until it cleared.

'It's the first time I've heard of a law that lets a man give you a bill one day and the next refuse to accept a cheque to pay the bill,' he said.

'My cheque is as good as any other in the country. I have £500 with the Board of Control. What about ringing the president of the Commonwealth Bank? He'll tell you my cheque is all right.'

After Dimitro and the Americans left, *The Sun* newspaper – who had labelled him a 'shoestring promoter' before he got here – had another go at the end of the tour.

As far as the paper was concerned, the promoter was 'an adventurer who thought he saw a chance of making some quick money out of a bunch of Australian suckers'.

Journalist Alan Hull blasted the 62-41 flogging as 'the greatest farce in the history of the game' with 'thousands of disgusted spectators' walking out before full time. He also alleged the Americans – with the knowledge of the Australian Board of Control – tried to pass off substitute local league players as Americans. In a fixture against Riverina at Gundagai, the All-Stars added at least four 'second-rate Sydney players' and then 'hid the identity of the replacements under the names of their own teammates and endeavoured to hoodwink the spectators into believing the players were All-Stars'.

It also noted Dimitro's parting comments about plans to give league a foothold in the States. 'It is nearly impossible to establish rugby league in America,' he said. 'The best we can do is keep in contact with the All-Stars when we get home so we can play exhibition matches when needed.'

Which was a far cry from the promises made when the team arrived just over a month earlier.

HE ADDED THAT WILSON WOULD BE A 'GOOD BOY' IF PENRITH SIGNED HIM. 'WE DO BELIEVE WE CAN HANDLE ANY PLAYER WE HAPPEN TO SIGN.'

16

A VERY BAD YEAR

The 1966 season wasn't the best for Balmain hooker Dick Wilson. He signed with the club in 1960 and in 1963 played in the grand final team that went down to St George 11-6. That year he was also chosen for the NSW side playing one game.

Before the start of the 1966 season, Wilson told the club he was retiring; the decision likely prompted by the club's refusal to put him on the transfer list so he could play with Manly. A week out from Round 1, Wilson told Balmain he was going to take action if they didn't let him go. At that time Manly secretary Ken Arthurson came out to deny he'd been having a few quiet words with Wilson.

'Everyone knows that this player's name has been linked with my club,' Arthurson said. 'In fact we have asked Balmain if they would be prepared to put him on a transfer fee. But I give my word of honour that Manly have not made him any offer or guaranteed that we would pay any actual transfer fee.'

Wilson was also eying off a move to country league club Tumut, one of eight clubs that broke away from Country Rugby League and so could snaffle him without worrying about transfer rules. 'This is something that could snowball,' Balmain secretary Kevin Humphreys said, 'with any player having a dispute with his club going to the breakaway area.'

With the Tigers not bending, Wilson chose to sit out the start of the season. It wasn't until three games in that he and Balmain patched things up and he agreed to return to training. 'I have thought it over and without any doubt this is the best move for me,' Wilson said. 'I had a good offer to play for Tumut in the breakaway group but I knocked it back.' After a week in third grade against Souths, he won back his hooker position for the Round 6 match against Parramatta.

It was shaping up to be a very good season for Balmain; they had won their first five games and wouldn't drop one until Round 12, when Canterbury beat them 15-11. From there things got a bit shaky; including that game against the Berries, Balmain lost six of their last seven games. But they were so far ahead of everyone except the Dragons, that they ended the season in second spot.

One of those losses ended up being very problematic for Wilson, who was dropped for the Round 16 match against Parramatta because he didn't turn up to training during the week. In Round 18, they lost to Newtown 8-6, and the club suspended Wilson a few days later, after he didn't show up for a committee meeting to answer allegations of conduct 'prejudicial to the best interests of the club'.

'In all fairness to the player I cannot say any more,' Humphreys told the media. 'You can ask as many questions as you like, but I can't give you any answers.' The club wouldn't be drawn on what Wilson did. But that just piqued people's curiosity to find out what happened. And what happened was gambling; Wilson, apparently on behalf of a friend, had negotiated a bet for Newtown to beat his own team, Balmain. In that game, Newtown's Clarrie Jeffreys dominated him in the scrums 13-6. He may not have intentionally played poorly to increase the chance of the bet paying off, but the defeat in the scrums definitely didn't help his cause.

The whole thing dragged on so long that not only did Wilson miss the last-round match against Wests, the club also held him out of the major semi against St George. The reason he missed the semi was an odd one; Wilson hadn't given the club his home address. The club constitution required a player to be given seven days' notice if he is called to answer charges but without his home address, they couldn't post the notification to him.

The club could only hand the notification to him when he appeared before a special committee, and the semi fell within that seven-day period. Wilson's solicitor thought that ridiculous and asked that the hearing be expedited. And so it was; the hearing took place the Monday before the semi-final and the club expelled Wilson and gave him an open transfer, meaning another club could sign him without having to pay the Tigers a transfer fee.

Penrith – which would debut in the league in the 1967 season – was pretty keen; the day after Wilson was expelled, the Panthers started sniffing around. 'We will investigate the circumstances arising from the Balmain inquiry,' Penrith club secretary Merv Cartwright said. 'If we feel it is only an internal problem, we might do something about Wilson.'

A week later, things still weren't clear. 'We don't know what went on between him and the Balmain club,' Cartwright said.

He added that Wilson would be a 'good boy' if Penrith signed him. 'We do believe we can handle any player we happen to sign.'

Penrith didn't end up signing Wilson. Even if he did sign with Penrith, events in the off-season raised the chance he could have been in jail when the 1967 season kicked off. In late November, Wilson found himself in court charged with assault of three men – Wallace Copp, James Blackwood and Brian Mark. The incident happened when Wilson and bookie Richard Hawthorne were drinking at the Royal Oak Hotel at Double Bay. In court, he claimed they were rushing to the aid of a woman who was being assaulted by Blackwood. It was alleged Wilson had used half a house brick, which he denied. Though he claimed Blackwood had whacked him across the face with a baton. That resulted in Wilson laying his own charges of assault against the trio.

What was revealed in court was that Robyn Ann Jones, Hawthorne's girlfriend, had left the pub around 9.50 pm in Hawthorne's car. She returned a short while later and started honking the horn to get the men's attention. Copp and Blackwood were locals long aggrieved at the noise that came from the Royal Oak. Copp had gotten out of bed and went down to tell Jones to cut it out. Blackwood joined him soon afterwards. And that was when Wilson and Hawthorne came out of the pub.

Thinking Jones was being assaulted, they ran to the car. Wilson claimed Blackwood had opened the car door and was trying to get inside. So Wilson yanked him out. 'He threw his left arm at me and I was struck on the chest,' Wilson testified in court. 'He was taller than I and I hit Blackwood with my fist on the right shoulder. He was finished. He did not want any more and he retreated.'

By then a third man, Brian Mark had turned up, and Wilson claimed he reached into the car – so the former Balmain player punched him in the face. A witness claimed Mark had an iron bar and hit Wilson in the face with it.

In late January, Wilson and Hawthorne were cleared of seven assault charges, but pleaded guilty to those remaining charges against Blackwood, Copp and Mark. Wilson then withdrew his assault charges against the trio and was ordered to pay $321 in court costs (just over $4000 in today's money).

In March the pair heard their sentence. They managed to avoid jail time, getting a three-month suspended sentence for each of the charges and were placed on a two-year good behaviour bond.

Wilson, by the way, never played football in the Sydney competition again. On the bright side, during the court case, Robyn and Richard got married.

A KID WHO IS JUST SIX AT THE START OF THEIR RUN IS ALMOST OLD ENOUGH TO VOTE BY THE TIME IT'S OVER.

17

THE END

The average age a kid starts following footy is around six. So take a hypothetical six-year-old who has just fallen in love with league. Imagine that child is back at the start of the 1956 season, where he or she has to pick a team to support.

Maybe if they're mercenary, they choose South Sydney – after all they had won the last three premierships and if you're going to pick a team, pick a winner, right? Maybe they pick the team Dad supported, or the team that represents the suburb they live in. The point is, whoever they pick, it's not St George.

Now, because of that decision made by a six-year-old, they would turn 17 before they saw a team that wasn't St George winning the grand final. They would have gone all the way through their primary schooling and almost finished high school before some other team won. Ironically enough, that team would be South Sydney.

That's the real-world way of looking at the Dragons' 11-in-a-row between 1956 and 1966. A kid who is just six at the start of their run is almost old enough to vote by the time it's over.

And around 4.25 pm on Saturday, 9 September 1967, it was over. Canterbury had managed to come from 9-0 down in the final to beat the Dragons 12-11. For those who could read it, the writing was on the wall two weeks out from the finals, when the Berries knocked over the Dragons 18-14. That was the first time the blue-and-whites had beaten the Dragons since 1953.

St George went into the finals as minor premiers with 16 wins. Only a point from a 12-all draw against Manly in Round 1 separated them from second-placed Souths, who they faced in the major semi-final – between the two of them, they'd won 16 of the last 17 grand finals (by the end of the 1971 season, that would have increased to 21 of the past 23 deciders).

Souths won that game – and the week off – 13-8 thanks to the accurate boot of Eric Simms. The Dragons scored two tries to Souths' one but Sims potted four from five (Kevin Longbottom also kicked one) to Dennis Preston's one-from-five.

After the match, Souths coach Clive Churchill said he would rather face Canterbury than the Dragons in the grand final. But he also hinted the Dragons would be hard-pressed to make the decider, telling the *Herald* he felt they'd have a hard time saddling up for next week's decider. *Herald* writer Phil Wilkins also thought the Dragons' time had come. 'The fiery breath burned low yesterday,' he wrote. 'After 11 seasons of scorching the ambitions of allcomers, the Dragons don't have to be told by their best friends. The mighty packs of the past are memories and the genius of its backline individuals could not gleam from the muddied arena yesterday.'

The lead-up to the final against Canterbury wasn't ideal for John Raper, who had a car accident two days before the game. On the same day, centre Bruce Pollard overslept and almost missed training (he started work at 4 am and had taken a nap before training). He turned up at Kogarah Oval just before the selectors ruled him out of the game.

On the other side of the field come game day was former St George hardman Kevin Ryan, who had left the Dragons for Canterbury because he was keen to coach. He would have stayed at the Dragons after the end of the 1966 season, but for a snub he received from the committee. After the season he arranged to meet with the committee to discuss his future. He spent an age waiting outside the committee room doors. 'Then finally someone emerged from the room,' Ryan told Larry Writer, 'and said to me "look, we know you're hanging on here, but we have other matters to attend to before we can get around to you". Isaid, "sorry, fellas. You've lost me".'

And so he took up the Berries' offer to captain-coach, even though the money they were offering was 'chickenfeed' (though Canterbury did have to pay St George a transfer fee, as per the rules at the time). Losing Ryan would be a major reason for the end of the Dragons' reign; he increased his new team's fitness via a gruelling St George-like pre-season and adopted the Red V's straight-line defence.

Still, the Dragons led the final 9-0 after 23 minutes and it seemed as though they were going to coast away to a win. But the Berries came back to lead 10-9 at the break. For all the talk of how Ryan stiffened their defence, it was the Berries attack that was the big improvement on the 1966 season; they scored 349 points in '67, compared to 244 a year earlier.

The second half got increasingly frantic, with the Dragons going up 11-10 via a Preston penalty goal before George

Taylforth kicked one from midfield for a 12-11 scoreline. The Dragons' team looked out of sorts with dropped balls and wild passes seen far too often. As the final minutes ticked away, the passing got even more frantic from the Dragons as everyone looked to someone else to snatch the game out of the fire – but no one did.

When the final siren sounded, the crowd let out what sounded like a loud cheer according to the game-day film, which contradicts the oft-told story that the stands were full of people weeping or in shock. When you think about it, it's quite likely a lot of people like that kid who was six in 1956 turned up for the chance to see the Dragons go out. Because, when we look back at that era, we tend to forget there were a load of other teams whose supporters had to put up with St George winning every year.

After the game, some Canterbury and St George players exchanged jerseys as though it was a grand final. Game-day footage showed the Dragons walking off the field while the Berries players stood and hugged. But they weren't being bad sports, the Dragons players were just lining up alongside the race that led to the Berries dressing sheds to applaud the victors from the field.

Not surprisingly the Dragons' loss made the front page of the Sunday papers. 'Tears shed as Saints bow out' read page one of *The Sun-Herald*. 'Emotional scenes marked the end yesterday of St George's 11-year reign as the premier team of Sydney rugby league,' Alan Clarkson wrote. 'St George's club secretary Frank Facer admitted weeping when Canterbury defeated his team 12-11 in the final at the SCG. It wasn't from remorse but pride for the way our boys went down fighting and then lined up to applaud Canterbury off the field.'

The front page also featured a photo of Kevin Ryan soaking in a bath while drinking from a celebratory bottle of champagne. At some stage, he had gone into the Dragons' dressing rooms to console his former teammates. 'I don't like seeing them go down,' he said. 'I'm so proud to have shared in their era'.

So what were the reasons the Dragons' run ended at 11? The introduction of the four-tackle rule usually gets the blame, with the claim it was introduced specifically to stop the St George juggernaut. That's a big ask, given the four-tackle rule was created in England in 1966. The brainchild of official Bill Fallowfield, he based it on American football's rule of allowing an attacking team four downs to advance the ball. If they fail, then they have to give up possession.

The NSWRL had little option but to introduce the new rule, which it did on a trial basis during the Wills Cup pre-season competition, where it was a success with spectators. So the league delegates voted to end unlimited tackle football and replace it with four-tackle footy. Showing some foresight, St George delegate Len Kelly moved an amendment that a team get six tackles rather than four. It was resoundingly voted down 34-6 (though, in a tacit admission that Kelly was right, the league increased it to six tackles for the 1971 season).

The St George officials didn't seem to have any concern that the four-tackle rule would be a problem, nor did media coverage make much of the idea of it being introduced to end St George's chances. Besides, every team would have to deal with the issue of how to play under the new rules. The ladder at the end of the regular season suggested St George were still competitive; the Dragons were minor premiers, scoring more points than anyone else and only three teams leaked fewer points than the Dragons.

They struggled early, with a first-round draw to Manly and then a surprise loss to newcomers Penrith in Round 4. But they hit their stride in the middle of the season, rattling off eight straight wins. There were a few concerns under the surface with the scorelines though. The Dragons' average scoreline was 19.8 to 12, which was easily the club's smallest average victory margin since they started winning premierships. It was in defence where the problem lay, the average of 12 points a game was the most since 1958.

The Dragons of 1967 were an ageing, injured lot. Captain Ian Walsh was 34, five-eighth Brian Clay was 33 and Raper and Reg Gasnier were 28.

Clay was keen to rack up 200 games, which would happen in the final. So that may have coloured his view of the knee injury he carried into the game. 'I am fit to play – fit to play my life out for the Saints,' Clay said. 'If I didn't think that way I wouldn't be playing. I've never let the Saints down yet and I don't intend to.' Walsh later admitted Clay shouldn't have played in that game. 'Sentiment got in the way of hard decision-making,' he told Writer, 'and I stuck up for him at the selection meeting even though I knew he couldn't step or swerve at all.'

Raper – who agreed Clay should not have played – had aggravated his back in the last-round match against Newtown, Facer ordering him to spend a week in a private hospital.

Once there, the injury was found to be worse than first thought and Raper stayed in traction and only made it to training a day or two before the final – and that car accident didn't help matters.

Langlands was also hurt, getting painkillers to deal with agroin injury. 'The needle was big and ugly,' Raper remembered, 'and he'd scream with pain when the doctor hit him with it.'

Not helping the injury concerns was the longer season, brought on by the admission of Penrith and Cronulla. The two new sides meant the Dragons had to play an extra four games in 1967, creating more wear and tear on those ageing bodies.

The two new teams also caused another serious problem for the Dragons. Cronulla took away some of the territory that had been St George's as well as some of their lower-grade players. In years gone by, the Dragons had an embarrassment of playing riches; if a top grader was injured or past his best, there was a lower grader ready to slot right in and keep the juggernaut going. But that wasn't the case anymore. Tellingly, neither of the Dragons' lower grades made the finals in 1967.

Now they had an ageing pack with no quality players to slip into the ranks to replace those lost through retirement or changing clubs. The officials had tried to replace Ryan with a new hard man in Queenslander John Wittenberg but were stung by a rule that players changing states had to sit out for a year.

Even if the Dragons had made it through to the final, it's highly likely Souths would have put them to the sword. Counting the major semi, the Dragons had lost to the Bunnies three times in 1967 and the cardinal and myrtle was a rising power. They'd gone from equal sixth with nine wins in 1966 to second place on 16 wins a year later – and their for and against was on a par with the Dragons'.

More crucially, the Souths' side had the benefit of youth. Most of the side – which included names like Ron Coote, John Sattler, Bob McCarthy, Eric Simms and John O'Neill – were in their early to mid-20s. They were in a position to return to their premiership-winning ways that were interrupted by St George in 1956. And they did, winning four of the next five grand finals – finishing runners-up in the one year they missed out on the big prize.

As a footnote, there was one St George player who would be on the field for the 1967 grand final day at the SCG. That would be fullback Graeme Langlands, who was there to pick up his new Ford Falcon 'De Luxe Sedan' for winning *The Sun*'s best and fairest competition. While a free car is always nice, Langlands probably wanted to leave the SCG turf with a very different grand-final day prize.

18

THE TRIALS OF DENNIS TUTTY

It may be hard to believe but, once upon a time, if you signed a contract to play for a particular team you were likely stuck with them for your entire playing career. Even after the contract you signed had expired.

Welcome to the transfer system, which was in place right up until the end of the 1971 season, when the efforts of Balmain Tiger Dennis Tutty saw the end of it. Back then a player signed with a club and effectively remained its property once the contract had expired. If the club wanted to keep a player after that point, all it had to do was add his name to the list of 'retained' players.

It was a rule that was written into the NSWRL Constitution and Rules. Here's rule 30, clause C: a player who signs as a professional player should note carefully that he is in effect tied to his club and cannot subsequently sign for any other club unless he is released – either by transfer or by the club agreeing to strike his name from their list of registered players.'

Sure, a player could request a transfer to another club – but the team that 'owned' him would place a price on his head which any other club had to pay. That money didn't go to the player but to the club – to modern eyes it seems not a million miles away from the buying and selling of slaves. And of course, the club could simply say no to the transfer request – and many did. As rule 30, clause F at the time stated, 'Unless the club agrees in writing that the player's name shall be removed from their list of registered players at a stated time then the club is entitled to retain the player's name on its register indefinitely.'

And this is where we meet the second rower named Tutty. He'd played for the Tigers under contract for the 1964–67 seasons and represented Australia in the First Test against New Zealand (there's a reasonably well-known photo of him, hands clasped in prayer in the Kangaroo line-up before kick-off). He played in the 1964 grand final against the Dragons – the only decider he would play in.

At the start of the 1968 season and in the last year of his contract, Tutty asked for a decent sign-on bonus – which he was entitled to, given his stellar performances over the previous two years. Balmain boss Kevin Humphreys (who would later be found guilty of defrauding the club) refused, so Tutty wrote to Humphreys asking for a transfer, only to be told again, no. So he lodged an appeal with the NSW Rugby League but withdrew before it was heard after speaking with Balmain coach Keith Barnes. To smooth things over, the Tigers offered him more money for his last season.

When the contract had expired, Tutty asked to be released to play elsewhere in 1969. Again, the answer was no. 'We will treat Dennis Tutty as we treat every other player,' Humphreys told the *Daily Mirror*. 'He can play with us under our terms and request a clearance at the end of the season. If Tutty makes himself available we'll decide what to do with him. We can't have players making ultimatums to us.'

This time he chose to sit out the 1969 season in protest. Surviving by working as a cleaner at Balmain Leagues Club, Tutty met up with David McKenzie, manager of the Australian fencing team and a solicitor. He advised Tutty to take the league to court.

But Tutty wasn't alone on that score – at least not at the start. Magpies winger John Elford and Tutty's Tiger teammate Peter Jones challenged the transfer system in the Equity Court in May 1969. Elford went to the courts before Tutty – he'd started proceedings by February, while Tutty took action a few months later.

Elford's lawyer told the court that 'he does not want to play for this club any longer and the consequence is that he cannot play for anyone. He wants to extricate himself from this position.' He'd asked for a transfer in previous years and even offered to play the 1968 season for Wests for free if they let him leave at the end of the year (as an aside, he also told the court of teammates turning up to training drunk and vomiting on the field).

Elford's efforts came to nought with Justice Hardie upholding the transfer system in August 1969. Despite the animosity, the following year he would re-sign with the Magpies, playing through to 1976, becoming an Australian representative in 1972.

The adverse ruling did not dissuade Tutty who, in sitting out the 1969 season had missed out on the Tigers' premiership. He went before the Full Equity Court in May 1970 arguing the transfer system was a restraint of trade. In October that year, the court dropped the bombshell that the system which had been in place since the 1950s was illegal. The court ruled that it was clear the transfer system meant a player could only carry out his trade with the club with which he was registered.

'In our view this must be regarded as a restraint of trade,' the judgement stated. 'We see no reason why the right of a man to the economic benefit of his own skill should find an exception in the case of a skilled footballer.'

The court granted Tutty's requested injunction against the transfer rule. The league was given 28 days to get its house in order before the rule change came into force, after it had told the court a 'degree of chaos' would ensue if the rule was changed immediately. Ultimately, the league would seek to challenge the decision. In December it asked the High Court for leave to appeal the decision, which was granted. At that time, Tutty was so strapped for money he had to sell his car, having already headed interstate looking for higher-paying work.

The appeal meant the saga continued into the 1971 season. Tutty had decided to play for Balmain that year because he needed the cash, though not before he was assured it wouldn't jeopardise his case. At $200 a win and $60 a loss, he would have made just a few grand that year.

Sensing a change could be in the wind regarding the transfer system, a number of other players looked to sit out until the High Court made its decision. They included Arthur Beetson, who wanted to leave Balmain. Sensing the appeal might fail, the Tigers ultimately granted him a transfer so as to make some cash out of the transfer before the system ended. South Sydney players Ron Coote and Mike Cleary were also considering their options. 'A bloke would be silly not to sit out at this stage and I am open to any offer,' Cleary told the *Herald*.

The league's High Court defence boiled down to 'you want to play in our game, you follow our rules'. Tutty's lawyer said the league was a closed shop where 'a person has no right against the rules of restraint which are laid down'.

It wasn't until 13 December that the High Court handed down its decision. The league's appeal was thrown out, confirming the lower court's ruling that the transfer system was a restraint of trade. The court said that, while football was a sport, this did not mean a person paid to play was not engaged in employment. Therefore, the transfer rule that stopped a player from seeking a new employer (aka another club) was invalid.

'This is plainly a fetter on the right of a player to seek and engage in employment,' said Chief Justice Sir Garfield Barwick. 'It is not the point to say that the player may resign from the league. If he does resign, he may perhaps obtain employment as a labourer or as a cricketer but he will not be able to obtain employment as a professional rugby league footballer either in NSW or in a number of other places. The rules, in our opinion, operate as a restraint of trade.'

Tutty was relieved the three-year fight was over. 'I have beaten them,' he said. 'I am free. There is no way they can hold me now.' The Sydney clubs agreed to delay for a week the signing of any players freed by the decision while the league changed its constitution. But in the following weeks at least 35 players signed on with new clubs, including Bunnies John O'Neill, Ray Branighan and Bob Moses to Manly in time for the Sea Eagles' 1973 premiership.

After years of trying, Tutty also made a move. He signed with Penrith for the 1972–74 seasons (for a lower sign-on fee than other players, who were quick to reap what Tutty had sown) before moving to Easts in 1975 – where he missed his second shot at a grand final. A broken arm during the season ruled him out of the Roosters' 38-0 shellacking of the Dragons in the decider.

Surprisingly, Tutty returned to the Tigers for the 1976 season, his last in the top grade, and coached the Tigers in 1980.

Truly, every player who has since come on the scene and signed a big contract, or been able to shop themselves around to get top dollar, owes Tutty a deep debt of gratitude. While Tutty admitted someone was always going to challenge the transfer system, the facts are that it was him.

'He was the one who shook the tree and enabled its bounty to fall to others,' the University of Melbourne's Braham Dabscheck wrote. 'He received neither financial nor moral support from other rugby league players of his generation, apart from three colleagues at Balmain.

'He was not backed by a club desirous of obtaining his services or a players' association in a test case on behalf of all players. The long and drawn-out nature of his legal action, and the financial and emotional pressure it placed him under, resulted in the deterioration of his health.

'Dennis Tutty, a person with limited formal education, an unskilled worker with a limited income, objected to employment rules which restricted his rights and freedoms, and guided by a personal philosophy which he developed in responding to the circumstances of his life, took on the NSWRL and righted a wrong.'

19

WALKOUT

'We will go off'.

Those were the words reportedly uttered by North Sydney captain Ken Irvine that sparked a controversy in the first round of the 1970 season. Norths were away at Belmore Oval, playing Canterbury. Irvine, who had played for the Bears since 1958 and was chosen for the Australian side while playing there, had only been reinstated as captain a month earlier, resigning in 1967 because he believed it was 'almost impossible' to lead the team from the wing.

Coach Roy Francis, in his second year with the team, had different ideas and figured he was perfect for the job. It didn't take long for Irvine to prove him wrong.

A minute before the half-time break there was an on-field blow-up after Irvine dove on a loose ball, only to be kicked and kneed by a Canterbury forward. Norths lock John McDonell rushed in to help his captain, 'which was the signal for an all-in melee in which punches and kicks were exchanged,' reported the *Herald*'s Alan Clarkson.

Referee Keith Page only saw fit to dismiss McDonell for kicking, on the advice of the touch judge. The Canterbury forward who started it all stayed on the field, as did the rest of the Berries side.

Canterbury got the penalty but before fullback Peter Inskip could take the kick, Page called up Norths' John Payne over a bit of backchatting. Captain Irvine joined them, only to find himself being sent off. Having had enough, Irvine told his players to walk off the field – centres Owen O'Donnell and Denis Cubis and second rower Noel Cavanagh following him off. The trio was stopped on the sidelines by coach Francis and several Norths officials and urged to go back onto the field.

Despite being two men down, Norths made a real effort in the second half, only losing to their full-strength opponents 16-14. Understandably, the league took a dim view of Irvine's attempt to lead his players off the field. At a judiciary hearing, McDonell got two weeks for 'deliberate kicking', while Irvine was outed for a week for 'indecent language to the referee'.

But the judiciary didn't stop there. It also cited a number of Norths players and officials to appear before a full inquiry. According to the league, this was due to there being a number of discrepancies in the various reports tendered by the Norths club and match officials.

After that inquiry and a closed-door meeting, the league decided to cite Irvine and Cubis for misconduct. 'Allegations are that Irvine and Cubis were instrumental in attempting to call the North Sydney team off the field in protest,' the *Herald* reported. The club had insisted there was no walk-off at all; the other players simply came to the sidelines to seek instruction. That the club had also claimed they were just walking off for the half-time break didn't really help their cause at all.

Irvine himself denied Page's claims that he twice told the ref 'we'll all go off', insisting he had never indicated by word or gesture that his team should leave the field. But touch judge reports backed the ref, and league vice-president Ken Charlton was emphatic he had seen Irvine wave the players off the field.

Irvine was found guilty by a vote of 25-13 and banned for two weeks, while Cubis escaped with a not-guilty finding of 22-13. In what seems to be rather dodgy, Cubis' vote was by a show of hands, while Irvine's was by secret ballot – the league clearly not brave enough to let people see who voted against Irvine. The Canterbury delegate Eddie Burns certainly saw it that way, claiming some of his fellow committeemen were 'a weak lot' for calling for a secret ballot.

At the end of the 1970 season, Irvine and Francis had a falling-out and, when the club took the coach's side, the winger signed with Manly. That didn't work out well for Norths; before the kick-off to the 1971 season Francis had resigned to head back home to England.

The change worked out very well for Irvine; he was on the wing for the Sea Eagles' 1972 grand final win over Eastern Suburbs – his last game in league. And the referee in that last game? Keith Page, the man in the middle for that walk-off match.

HE COCKS HIS
RIGHT ELBOW
AND CANNONS
IT ACROSS
THE SOUTHS
PLAYER'S JAW.

20

SATTLER'S JAW

When you're watching the game, even though you know exactly what's going to happen, it still comes out of the blue. Maybe that's because the game footage on the league's official DVD is shot from a different angle to that clip online that you and so many others have seen. Maybe it's also because the former is in black and white, while the clip is in faded 1970s colour.

Or maybe it's because the violence comes with no announcement. The clip is solely of the incident itself. We already know what we're going to see; we're primed for it. However, watching the entire game is very different. Maybe through years of watching rugby league, we've come to expect that something that blatant, that nasty, must have been in retaliation for something. There must have been a dust-up, a brawl – a melee if you will – that happened earlier to explain it all.

But no. The Manly side kicks for touch after their fullback Bob Batty is hit high. Hooker Freddie Jones takes the tap and they run the same set piece with several decoy runners they used in a restart a few minutes earlier. In that earlier instance, the rangy Manly player with the mop of curly hair took the pass (but then he dropped it). So when the same play appears again, it makes sense that the Souths player – dressed in a slightly-too-tight jersey with the sleeves rolled up past his elbows as if to accentuate his muscular frame – zeroes in on him.

However, this time the curly-headed player doesn't get the ball. The South Sydney player still hits him on suspicion, more a body check than anything else, before turning his head away to watch the ball carrier get tackled. The Manly player turns to walk back to his side of the field. But, seeing the Souths player distracted, it's as though a thought suddenly pops into his head. He hadn't thought about doing this before he got on the field, but he cocks his right elbow and cannons it across the Souths player's jaw.

The Souths player staggers from the shock of the blow but, to his credit, remains on his feet. Then, as though the Manly player has thought 'in for a penny, in for a pound', he puts his rival in a headlock and gives his face a workout as if to ensure the damage intended by the elbow.

He then lets the Souths man go, and they both walk back to their teams. Meanwhile, the play continues, no other players show the slightest reaction and the referee Don Lancashire doesn't blow his whistle to caution anyone. In fact, it's over before the TV commentator can finish his sentence 'a fight's starting out already but Lancashire is allowing play to go on'.

Yes, it's the incident from the 1970 grand final where John Bucknall broke John Sattler's jaw just three minutes into the game. Though if you've only seen that video clip, you probably didn't know when it happened. And if you've only seen that clip, there's a whole story you've missed out on.

To wind the clock back a bit, it's worth pointing out that Sattler was not a cleanskin. A man with an acknowledged habit of getting hot under the collar, he didn't need directions to find the judiciary rooms. In 1963 he was sent off for fighting in a pre-season match against Manly. The following season, he was marched twice – for kicking and a stiff-arm tackle.

He was sent off again in 1965 and copped two weeks for 'deliberate tripping'. In the '67 season he had two weeks out for throwing punches and was sent off for decking Yorkshire prop Dave Hill in a Kangaroos tour match. Sattler regretted his actions in the Test but said he was retaliating after Hill let go with one too many elbows in the scrum.

In the 1968 season he was sent off and later cautioned for spitting in an opponent's face. Sattler's defence was that the other player spat in his face first, and he was merely returning the favour. He told the judiciary he was disgusted with the incident. 'I am only sorry I reacted the way I did,' he said. In 1969, he had an early shower in a NSW versus Queensland match for punching, only to escape with a caution from the judiciary.

In the 1970 season, he was still getting in hot water. In the Round 13 Souths-Parramatta match he was involved in an incident that sparked an all-in brawl. It started when he was tackled by Eels lock Rod Tolhurst. 'As the pair struggled on the ground, a couple of players came in and punches were thrown,' reported the *Herald*'s Alan Clarkson. 'This was the signal for the two teams to converge and the brawl was on in earnest. Punches were traded as the players milled around in a big group, with referee Les Samuelson and his touch judges powerless to stop them.'

Despite almost every player being involved, and the brawl being so bad *The Sun-Herald* decided to award no 3-2-1 votes from the game, no one was sent off. Sattler was one of a number of players cautioned, but the game continued with 26 players on the field. In Round 17, he was gone for standing on the arm of an opponent, but he said after the game it was an accident.

'Bobby McCarthy had tackled Walsh and I came over the top to make sure he was down,' Sattler told *The Sun-Herald*. 'In the scrimmage my boot definitely came in contact with Walsh's arm. But it was an accident. It was not done viciously.' The judiciary were having none of it; they suspended Sattler for two weeks.

On the other side of the equation, the week before the 1970 semi against Manly, Sattler saved an old man from being run over by a train at Jannali station. 'I was standing at the station talking to one of the members of the club committee when I heard people screaming "Stop the train, stop the train",' Sattler said.

I glanced towards the platform and saw a suitcase perched at the edge. When I rushed over I saw this poor old man trapped down there. He was unable to move.

'I reckon the old guy must have fainted. I jumped down, threw him back on to the platform before he could be killed.'

Saving a man from being hit by a train surely balances out the karma for any send-offs in the 1970 season.

There was an odd moment in that 1970 finals series. Souths dropped Bob Honan off the reserves bench for the semi-final against Manly three days before the game – because he refused to train in the rain. This came shortly after coach Clive Churchill had issued a 'no train, no play' edict to Souths' utility Paul Sait. Honan would return to the bench for the grand final.

In the Souths-Manly semi, it's possible Sea Eagles coach Ron Willey's words were echoing in the head of John Bucknall – he who owned the elbow that whacked Sattler's jaw. Seeing the Souths captain as a key player, he told Bucknall to get him off the field, to take him out. He probably stopped short of 'smash his jaw, Johnny boy', but the advice actually backfired. Sattler didn't leave the field.

But Manly did what they could to send him to the sidelines. For a few minutes, Sattler is justifiably unsighted in the match footage. But when he takes the first hit-up from a kick-off (Souths had scored to take a 3-0 lead), Bucknall is there to greet him with a stiff-arm aimed right at Sattler's sore spot. 'Sattler, he's been hit twice,' the commentator says. 'The first time Bucknall hit Sattler, the referee missed it.'

Other times Sattler takes the ball up – and he doesn't shy away from this – various Manly players swing arms or place him in a headlock and start twisting his jaw. So clearly Bucknall has put the word out to his teammates what happened.

In what would seem like a massive stroke of misfortune, every time a scrum packs, Sattler finds himself packing down directly opposite his attacker. But Sattler takes advantage of the closeness to hand out some retribution. In the first scrum after the elbow, Sattler ends up with Bucknall in a headlock and his hand covering his face. When they break up, Bucknall reaches up to check his face for blood, so Sattler has obviously given him something. The following scrums follow a similar pattern; when one collapses and Sattler finds Bucknall on the ground in front of his feet, he can't resist giving him a kick.

'There's some action on the blind side of the scrum,' the commentator says. 'The referee couldn't see that, it's Sattler and Bucknall. They're having quite a good time together today.'

At the same time, Sattler's Souths' teammates know what went on and make the rest of Bucknall's grand final a circus of pain. A few minutes after the incident, Bob McCarthy hits Bucknall with everything, causing him to lose the ball. Soon afterwards Bucknall is on his haunches getting treatment from the ambulance man; it's likely someone clipped him out of sight of the camera.

Later in the first half, McCarthy delivers a vicious backslam to Bucknall, while other Souths players look to whack him whenever he takes a hit-up. By this time, Bucknall looks like he's exhausted, in pain, and searching for a towel to throw in. After one whack too many, Bucknall stays down for treatment while Souths run in a try on his side of the field. Sims misses the conversion but Souths are up 10-4. And Bucknall is taken off the field; his plan has turned out exactly the opposite of what he had hoped.

From here to full time you know the story. In the sheds at half-time Sattler's teammates tell him he can't go back on. Sattler, who can be seen throughout the game pushing up his jaw to lock it in position, says he's fine and he's going back out. Souths win 20-12 and plenty of post-match photos of Sattler with his jaw hanging loosely are taken (a favourite is one with Churchill at his side with his right hand cupped in front of Sattler as though he's ready to catch the jaw should it fall free).

There was no hiding Sattler's injury from the press. The front page of *The Sun-Herald*'s sports section crowed 'Sattler ignores injury as Souths win'. 'South Sydney captain John Sattler led his team to victory in the rugby league premiership yesterday, playing with a probably fractured jaw for 70 minutes of the game,' the lead read.

Though the paper likely didn't know it, the picture with that story showed the jaw-breaking incident with Sattler and Bucknall. The pair are to the left of the picture, Bucknall's left arm wrapped around Sattler's head, who is trying to claw himself free. Oddly, it's not the most striking part of the image; on the right, Souths' John O'Neill is tackling an opponent, looking as though he's about to swing a right uppercut.

Inside, the coverage of Souths' third grand final in four seasons focused on Sattler's injury. 'Sattler was the centre of a couple of tough incidents early in the game and came out of one with blood caking his mouth,' Alan Clarkson wrote. 'Half a dozen of his teeth were snapped off and others were loosened in a head-high tackle. "I didn't see who did it," Sattler said. "Someone came around from behind and caught me."

'Sattler did not want to talk about the incident, but club officials suspected that his jaw was broken. He was a sorry sight in the dressing room as he lay back in a bath, with his front teeth broken and his jaw badly swollen.'

It wasn't true that he didn't know the culprit; the way he and other Souths players went for Bucknall throughout the first half, they all knew exactly what happened.

The most staggering thing out of all this is that Bucknall never spent a moment on the sideline for shattering Sattler's jaw. It was an era before post-match video review so if the referee and touch judges missed the transgression, the player got away with it. Everyone knew what had happened immediately after the game, and the hundreds of thousands who have seen the footage online since know who broke Sattler's jaw. Yet referee Lancashire didn't see anything – even though he was looking straight at the incident, so no one had to pay for Sattler's jaw. But the Souths captain has had plenty of time to get over the injury that made him a legend. 'Do I hate Bucknall?' he wrote in his autobiography. 'No, I don't. Have I forgiven him? Yes, I have. Would I rewrite history and erase the moment I broke my jaw? No, I wouldn't.'

21

THE LEAGUE-A-THON

Some say the NRL swiped the idea for its Magic Round – started in 2019 – from the UK Super League. Over there, they first played all matches in one place, calling it Magic Weekend, back in 2007.

But really, the idea of playing a weekend of footy at the same ground isn't new. The NSWRL came up with the 'Magic Round' concept almost half a century ago. Though they gave it the far less impressive name of 'League-A-Thon'. In 1977, over the Anzac Day long weekend all six Round 6 matches were played at the SCG, two each on Saturday, Sunday and Monday.

In what seems like a tacky (or egalitarian, take your pick) approach to ticket sales, people could buy them at certain supermarkets and bottle shops. Costing $2 for the hill and $3.50 for a grandstand seat, the tickets came with 'free food and grog vouchers', according to newspaper ads. Buy a grandstand ticket and you got $7 in vouchers that could be used at the supermarket or 'grog shop'. It was a pretty unimpressive deal; spend $20 at one of those places and you could use one of the vouchers to get a whole dollar off the price. As a deal, it worked better for the stores than it did the customer.

If you didn't buy a ticket, there was a great deal available; Channel Seven televised four of the six games. That was a big deal in an era where fans would be lucky to see more than one televised game a week.

As a concept League-A-Thon was the brainchild of advertising man and Newtown fan John Singleton. But, despite all the promotion that went on ahead of the weekend, the first day was a fizzer. Penrith and Balmain drew 19-all, while Canterbury defeated Souths 13-12. The 12,576-strong crowd that saw those games was well short of the 40,000 the league had expected.

'No round in the history of the code has received more publicity than this weekend,' wrote the *Herald*'s Alan Clarkson, 'but the league and the sponsors were dismayed at the attendance.'

Things had picked up by the holiday Monday, with a crowd of 32,463 on hand to watch Easts beat Manly 20-0 (in what was Bob Fulton's first match against Manly since switching to Easts) and Cronulla thump Newtown 37-10. 'Although the total attendance for the three days,' the *Herald* reported, 'was nearly 17,000 under last year's figure for the Anzac weekend the sponsors were satisfied with the venture and will be back next year.'

Singleton admitted he wished more people had shown up 'but everyone made money and the sponsors are delighted with the increase in liquor and food sales resulting from the series'.

It did return for the 1978 Anzac Day weekend, but with a tweak – there would be no games on the Saturday and triple-headers on Sunday and Anzac Day on the Tuesday. It was a big call from the league as there had been games on Saturdays for decades. It also started people wondering how much the league would charge to see three games in a day. Surprisingly, the games were cheaper than the year before – $2 for adults and kids and pensioners were free.

But the event wasn't free of problems. While they pulled in a big crowd of 44,507 on the Sunday, there had been long queues outside due to a shortage of functioning turnstiles and insufficient toilet facilities due to the construction of new grandstands.

League boss Kevin Humphreys said the problems would be fixed in time for the triple-header on the Tuesday Anzac Day holiday, but feared the adverse publicity would put people off heading to the SCG. And he was right – the crowd for that day was well down on Sunday's figure – just 25,004 came through the gates.

And that was it for the League-A-Thon. It didn't return for the 1979 season. The league wouldn't revisit the idea of triple-headers until the introduction of Magic Round in 2019. But they did give double-headers a go, most notably to kick-start the 1999 season. Round 1 of that season saw a Knights-Manly and Dragons-Newcastle double-header at Stadium Australia. You could say that concept was a success; it drew in a then world-record crowd for a league match of 104,583.

That record wouldn't even last the season; the 1999 Dragons-Storm grand final eclipsed it with a crowd of 107,999. A record that still stands today, though some claim the 1954 UK Challenge Cup replay drew much more than the official 102,569 crowd figure.

THEY TOOK PART IN, NOT ONE, NOT TWO, BUT THE THREE LOWEST-SCORING MATCHES IN PREMIERSHIP HISTORY.

22

THE LOW-SCORING JETS

They mightn't have played in the top grade for decades and there is now a generation of fans that have never heard of them, but there is a spot in the rugby league record books that will forever belong to the Newtown Jets. They took part in, not one, not two, but the three lowest-scoring matches in premiership history – managing to win two of them.

The one they didn't win was the lowest score of all time – and they didn't win because it was a nil-all draw. Newtown and Canterbury faced off at Henson Park on 28 March 1982 (the same day, incidentally, that the Swans played their first AFL match at their new Sydney home). There doesn't seem to be much in the way of match footage that has survived, which is probably not a bad thing given the scoreline is very suggestive of a bludger of a game.

After 80 minutes of football on a wet and overcast day, neither side was good enough to even manage to score a single point. While there were plenty of attempts, they mostly failed due to the ineptness of the attackers, rather than any degree of robust defence. After all, neither team would play finals football that season. A year after making the grand final Newtown finished in seventh place, four points out of the top five with the Bulldogs a point and place further behind.

The Jets bombed a try when Phil Sigsworth was put into the clear and on his way to the try line when the ref called the play back for a forward pass.

Just before half-time, Newtown kicker Ken Wilson missed a shot at goal. Canterbury's Tony Armstrong returned the favour early in the second half and halfback Steve Mortimer missed a field goal shot.

A decision by referee Barry Goldsworthy with six minutes on the clock caused its share of controversy. A scrum flared up right in front of Canterbury's posts the result of which saw Newtown prop Steve Bowden flattened by an opponent. Both touch judges ran in; one said Canterbury's Peter Cassilles was the aggressor, the other pointed the finger at Bowden. Rather than award a penalty to Newtown, he ordered a scrum to be packed – an odd decision after someone has been laid out.

Almost a decade earlier, in 1973, the Jets and Dragons met at the SCG for a Round 5 clash that became the second-lowest score in premiership history – a 1-0 win to Newtown. The immortal Jack Gibson was coach of the Jets for only that year, having previously led Easts and St George. Before this match, Gibson dragged out his favourite film – *Second Effort*. A 1968 sales training film featuring NFL coach Vince Lombardi, it's gained iconic status over years but, to be honest, really hasn't stood the test of time. Lombardi's efforts to compare sales to football are heavy-handed and he is a really wooden actor. The camerawork leaves a lot to be desired – so many shots are extreme close-ups of Lombardi's head and others are shot into the sun so both the coach and his salesman friend are in shadow.

Gibson was enamoured of its motivational nature and had already screened it for the Dragons. He felt it would be useful for the Jets because they didn't have any star players who could pour on the points, so if they were going to win any games they would have to focus on defence. So 'stop them scoring tries' became the Jets' mantra. And it worked; the previous season the team had let in 371 points but in 1973 that dropped to 224. In 11 matches – two of them in the finals – the Jets held their opponents to single figures.

That Round 5 match against the Dragons spelled out the Jets' style in 1973 – if you score one point, just make sure the opposition doesn't score any. The game was the 'worst seen at the Sydney Cricket Ground for years', according to the *Herald*'s Alan Clarkson. He said the Jets botched at least a half-dozen chances for tries. 'Play became so pathetic that the players were booed off the ground at half-time,' Clarkson wrote. 'But worse was to follow. The crowd started to laugh at some of the amateurish efforts of these "first-grade" players.'

Not that Gibson cared too much; he knew attack wasn't the Jets' key to victory. It was defence – you have to go with what you've got.

After 69 minutes, the scoreboard attendant really hadn't done anything at all. At that point, Gibson called on Ken Wilson (who also played in Newtown's 0-0 draw) – who had already played in third grade that afternoon – and who came on to kick a field goal.

After two plays and just 13 seconds after he got on the field, Wilson potted the one-pointer. But the match wasn't over; the Dragons still had a few chances to win the match. Winger John Chapman raced away along the touchline, only to be pulled down short of the try line by Newtown fullback John Floyd. Following the play-the-ball, referee Keith Page found Newtown off-side, giving the Dragons a shot at a penalty goal with just three minutes on the clock. Chapman's kick missed, but the Saints could have still snatched away a draw, with play inside the Jets' quarter in the dying seconds. The distance was close enough for Billy Smith to snap a field goal and walk away with a draw, but the full-time hooter sounded before he had the chance.

That year, Newtown finished in the top five on 28 points and their 1973 season was stopped one match short of the grand final in a 20-11 loss to Cronulla. Still, Newtown's turnaround was enough for Gibson to be named the league's coach of the year.

For the next lowest game, we have to go all the way back to 1914 and a 2-0 win to Newtown over Eastern Suburbs. It was a wet, rainy Saturday afternoon but that didn't stop around 14,000 turning out to watch the game. Shelter was obviously high on their agenda; photos from the match show the roofed stand is full, while the hill on the other side is almost empty.

On the field for Easts was Dally Messenger's lesser-known brother Wally. But don't feel sorry for him living in the shadow of a famous brother; Wally played in two premiership-winning sides and was picked for the Kangaroos in 1914. So he did all right.

But he didn't do all right in this messy game against Newtown. Messenger missed several attempts at field goal, as well as a sitter of a penalty goal from right in front late in the first half. The only score of the match came earlier in that half, via a penalty goal from Newtown winger Charlie Russell.

Messenger had a similar amount of chances in the second half to put points on the board but, with the rain coming down heavier than in the first, he had no chance. 'Eastern Suburbs were having plenty of opportunities to equalise the scores,' Sydney's *The Sun* reported, 'for once again Messenger missed the goal'.

It just wasn't Messenger's day – nor was it the day of Eastern Suburbs. They finished on the wrong side of a very low score. Though, as we have seen, Newtown would go even lower.

IF YOU'RE GOING TO COACH A RUGBY LEAGUE TEAM, IT REALLY HELPS TO HAVE YOUR HEAD AROUND ALL THE RULES.

23

THE REPLACEMENTS

If you're going to coach a rugby league team, it really helps to have your head around all the rules. That sounds incredibly obvious but some teams have had to wear the punishment for their coach getting it wrong. That's quite evident when they get things wrong while replacing a player.

In the 1988 Anzac Day match against Manly at Brookvale, Souths coach George Piggins thought he'd give lower-grade player Scott Wilson a reward by throwing him on in garbage time. After all, Souths had the game won at 28-14. Wilson was a shining light in the lower grades; he had toured England with the Australian Schoolboys in 1986 at just 15, was a star in the Under 23s, and was picked for reserve grade at just 16. That Anzac Day afternoon, Piggins tapped him on the shoulder to ride the bench for first grade, getting on the field for the last six minutes.

But there was a problem. Having played in the Presidents Cup match earlier that day, under NSWRL rules, Wilson wasn't eligible to be used as a replacement in the top grade. That meant Souths were facing the loss of their two competition points.

Amazingly, this was but one issue in a controversial match. Four players were sent to the sin bin after a brawl erupted 18 minutes into the game. Later, Manly coach Bob Fulton directed captain Paul Vautin to tell referee Bill Harrigan that an official complaint would be lodged over his performance (this was a year after Fulton had infamously told Harrigan he hoped he was run over by a cement truck). Also, the league pledged to look into the use of walkie-talkies on the field after Vautin received the order from Fulton via a radio brought onto the field by a trainer.

In terms of Souths' screw-up regarding the replacement rule, it didn't look good for the Bunnies. The league had actually sent out a reminder to every club just three days before the Souths-Manly clash. In the days after the incident, Piggins admitted he didn't read the league directives, saying he wasn't 'a Rhodes scholar'.

'If I think some correspondence is important I hand it to my wife,' he told the *Herald*. 'But I'm only doing this coaching job for a sandshoe and a galosh and I don't think I should have to pay my wife to read all the correspondence coming in from the NSWRL about rules.' That a coach doesn't look to keep up to date on the rules is a very strange admission to make.

Piggins, who admitted he 'goofed', wasn't helped by Souths' practice of only completing team sheets after the game, rather than before – and then not including the players on the bench. As league supremo John Quayle said, if they'd completed the team sheets properly before the game, Wilson sitting on the bench for Firsts would have been picked up and the league then would notify Souths that wasn't allowed – and that would have been the end of it.

Instead, the NSWRL ruled that Souths had to lose their two points, which Piggins thought was really rather unfair. 'I feel like a bloody idiot for doing it but I find it hard to believe that the league could take two points off the team for such a little thing,' he said. 'What would have happened had we lost? Obviously we would have been fined, which means there are two different penalties for a similar offence. The punishment for such a nothing crime is far too severe as far as I'm concerned.'

Yes, that is true, but a losing team has no points to take away as punishment so a fine has to stand as a substitute. Also, when breaching the replacement rule has the potential to alter the course of a game, to let a team retain the points doesn't make sense. In this case, the match was over before Wilson took the field, but there realistically has to be a consistent rule across all games.

At least in Souths' case the loss of the two points didn't have greater ramifications for their season. They finished six points out of the top five, so even with those two points, they still wouldn't have made the finals.

In other cases, a mix-up over replacements has cost teams dearly. In 2009, one cost the Bulldogs $100,000. In a Round 2 match against the Panthers, the Dogs snatched a 28-26 win in the 78th minute, via a converted try from Ben Roberts. But there was a problem – when he touched down Canterbury had 14 players on the field.

That was the result of quite a screw-up with replacements. Roberts had come on as a late replacement for Andrew Ryan, who went off on the far side of the field. Then hooker Mick Ennis went down with injury, the trainer called Ryan back onto the field and he was in the attacking line when Roberts scored. On top of that, Ryan was never meant to leave the field; Roberts was supposed to replace Greg Eastwood, who left the field after the try was scored but wasn't replaced.

At issue was the Dogs had ignored the interchange rule that requires a player to hand a card to an official before being allowed onto the field – it's a rule designed to avoid exactly this situation happening.

The league only picked up on the transgression by chance. In post-match coverage on Fox, questions were raised about the Roberts-Ryan interchange. The league watched replays and confirmed that it was all above board. 'In the process, however,' said NRL chief operating officer Graham Annesley, 'it became clear that after Andrew Ryan left the field and was walking away from the play, he then appeared to be called back on by a trainer. There are clearly 14 men on the field when the try is scored.'

League boss David Gallop decided to take away the Dogs' two points for the breach of the interchange rule. Canterbury coach Kevin Moore said the team would take it on the chin and not look to blame anyone. 'From time to time we all make mistakes,' he said. 'We learn from it, move on and all stick together.'

Bulldogs CEO Todd Greenberg said the team would appeal the result, claiming 'the two points should be ours'. It was to no avail, the NRL would not be moved. In a cheeky move, Panthers CEO Michael Leary felt, if the points weren't the Bulldogs' then they should be Penrith's. 'The NRL has decided to take the two competition points from the Bulldogs, so they're saying the fact they had 14 men on the field influenced the result of the game. Who's to say the try would have been scored if they'd only had 12 against 13?' It was an approach that was doomed to fail, simply because the league never overturned the result of the game. Besides, Penrith *didn't* win the game – so they didn't deserve the two points.

Giving up those two points came back to dog the Dogs in the tail-end of the year. That season there was a tussle between Canterbury and St George Illawarra for the minor premiership. In the penultimate round the Dragons dropped their game against Souths, while the Dogs beat the Warriors putting them in the top spot for the first time since Round 11. Going into the final round, there were two possibilities for awarding the JJ Giltinan Shield; if the Dogs won against the Tigers at the Sydney Football Stadium, it was theirs. But if they lost and the Dragons beat Parramatta at Kogarah, then it would go to St George Illawarra.

With both games on the Friday night, it created a headache for CEO Gallop, who started out at the Canterbury game with the shield, only to have to rush to Kogarah when it became clear the Dogs were going to blow their chance and lose to the Tigers.

The table at the end of the final round had the Dragons and Dogs tied on 38 points, but the Red V got the shield because of a better for and against. But had Canterbury not lost those two points back in Round 2, they would have finished on 40 points, winning the minor premiership – and the $100,000 in cash that came with it.

While they didn't lose a wad of cash, the 1975 Western Suburbs Magpies paid dearly for a mistake with a replacement during a game at Belmore against Canterbury in Round 15. With nine minutes to go, Wests were up 7-5 but Canterbury's Graeme Hughes snatched a draw with a 40-metre penalty goal.

In the 34th minute of the game, Wests' bench forward Mick Liubinskas replaced second rower Jim Murphy. Liubinskas had ridden the bench in reserve grade that day, only getting on in the last 10 minutes. That was a problem for Wests; any first-grade reserve had to play a full game in reserves to be eligible. So according to the law, Liubinskas was an illegal replacement. There was no question of him affecting the score – he scored Wests' only try in the game.

Canterbury protested to the league, which saw Wests docked the one point for a draw. To their credit, the Berries' delegate on the league committee refrained from voting on any motion related to the challenge.

'It was all done in innocence … we did not know the rule,' claimed Wests' secretary Dudley Beger. It was a stance that drew criticism from some in the media. 'That a club would not have known one of the cardinal rules of the game, a rule that has been in operation for six years, is indefensible,' wrote the *Herald*'s Alan Clarkson.

Calling the replacement rule a 'cardinal rule' of league was a real reach by Clarkson. He was on much more solid ground when he noted Wests were told of their error before half-time, with the Magpies down 5-0. They left Liubinskas on the field, believing the replacement rule meant a player had to 'complete' a game to be eligible for first grade, rather than having to play a 'complete game'.

Losing that single point hit the Magpies hard at the back end of the season. After the last round, they were caught up with Parramatta and Balmain in a three-way tie for fifth spot on 21 points. In an era before the league used points differential to split tied teams, a series of play-offs were called for. On Tuesday, Western Suburbs had to rock up to the SCG to take on Parramatta, with the winner to back up against Balmain on the Thursday. No matter who won, playing two mid-week games isn't the best preparation for a semi-final that weekend.

It was Parramatta who took fifth spot, knocking over Wests and then Balmain, before also winning their semi against Manly on Sunday. But the play-offs could have been avoided. Had Wests not lost that single point in Round 15, they would have finished the regular season in outright fifth place on 22 points. With the finals experience of the previous year, where Wests made it all the way to the preliminary final, the Magpies might have been able to go a step further in 1975. But not knowing just one rule ended up costing them a finals spot.

‘THERE IS SOMETHING INHERENTLY DANGEROUS ABOUT PLAYERS LAYING THEIR HANDS ON REFEREES.’

24

WHAT A TACKLE

When it comes to touching a referee, Balmain's Steve Roach is the poster boy. Plenty of people remember him giving Eddie Ward a patronising pat on the head after being sin binned in a 1990 match against Manly at Brookvale. To make absolutely sure he had booked a date at the judiciary, he called the touch judge a 'fucking wombat' as he walked off.

At Monday night's judiciary hearing chairman Dick Conti was not impressed. 'There is something inherently dangerous about players laying their hands on referees. It is of great concern in terms of the example it sets for junior players, especially since it was the television match.' For his sins Roach got four weeks and a $5000 fine.

A year later another player would receive a longer sentence for handling a referee. A sentence many thought was undeserved. In a 1991 Round 4 match between Souths and Newcastle, Rabbitohs second rower Wayne Chisholm got in trouble for tackling referee Geoff Weeks. Now, it's not as bad as it sounds. Newcastle's John Schuster had evaded two defenders and was heading towards the try line, he ran close to Weeks as Chisholm came into the picture, eyes only for Schuster. But with the referee in the way, he ended up taking Weeks down instead – though the ref bounced back up straight away, uninjured. 'Weeks was dead centre between Chisholm and Schuster and took the full brunt of the tackle as the Knights winger raced on for the try,' the *Herald*'s match day report read.

Many agreed with that assessment; Chisholm hadn't intended to tackle Weekes, the referee was just in the wrong place at the wrong time. With so much happening on a league field, it's actually to the credit of the refereeing ranks that this hardly ever happens. Generally they manage to stay out of the way of the play.

The league didn't see it the same way as most fans. The following day Chisholm was charged with 'misconduct, in that he sought to gain an advantage for himself by physically interfering with the referee'.

At the hearing touch judge Gary Lee said he did not believe Weeks had gotten in Chisholm's way and in goal judge Barry Ruttle claimed Chisholm 'deliberately ran into the referee'. Chisholm's representative Jim Poultis asked the officials, if it was that bad, why didn't they report it to Weeks immediately? As it was, the charges didn't arise until the following day when Weeks himself saw a replay of the incident and submitted his report.

Despite the fact that it appeared to be an accident, the judiciary decided to punish Chisholm. 'The panel has concluded that it cannot accept Mr Chisholm's evidence that he didn't see the referee,' Conti said in the judiciary ruling.

'We think he must have seen him. There was no intention to injure the referee. Obviously if that had been the intention, the offence would have been in an entirely different category.

'We believe the contact was made knowingly, but more out of frustration than design.'

He was outed for a massive 10 weeks and wouldn't return to the field until Round 15. That sentence didn't look right when compared to Roach's punishment. The Balmain prop handled a ref and abused a touch judge – both intentionally – but got just four weeks. Chisholm's tackle was an accident but he copped more than twice as many weeks on the sideline.

It made some wonder which player got off lightly. Souths officials thought it might have been Chisholm, not wanting to risk appealing and copping a longer sentence. 'You knock a referee down in a tackle and get 10 weeks? I think we'd be inclined to go quietly about that,' an unnamed Souths official said.

THAT LEFT A ONE-HOUR GAP IN WHICH NINE PLANNED TO SCREEN A GAME THAT WENT FOR 80 MINUTES.

25

FREE THE 33

These days footy fans are spoiled by TV coverage. We can watch every game of the weekend live via a number of different platforms and now, even the pre-season trials turn up on the box. But it wasn't always that way. Back in the day the best you could hope for was two weekend matches: one on the ABC on Saturday afternoon and a Sunday night game on whichever commercial station had the rights.

It got even worse in the 1990s, when footy fans got what was effectively one and a half games. That was because Channel Nine took the rights to rugby league from Channel Ten in 1992. Channel Nine insisted the Sunday night schedule wouldn't change to fit in the footy. That meant the news would stay at 6 pm and *60 Minutes* at 7.30 pm.

That left a one-hour gap in which Nine planned to screen a game that went for 80 minutes. Execs at Channel Ten, where the Sunday league coverage went for an hour and a half, were snickering. 'The league has been on an excellent wicket at Ten and is about to find out what it's like taking what they can get,' one exec told *The Sun-Herald*.

When the 1992 season came around, fans quickly realised how little league they got from Nine. Remember the one-hour blocked out for league included ads, which left a bit over 40 minutes of footy. What the channel did was screen edited highlights.

The move sparked howls of protest in NSW and Queensland. Brisbane's Val Gadd was one of a number of people who started a petition over the poor coverage. By the start of the season, she'd already collected 10,000 signatures. 'I know people who are going off the game altogether,' she said. 'They don't turn Channel Nine on anymore, and they're not watching their football.'

Nine tried to justify their decision by noting the Round 1 Canberra-Penrith match in the one-hour format rated higher than the 1991 season opener of Wests-Balmain – 580,000 viewers versus 365,000. Gee, who'd have thought a rematch of the previous season's grand finalists would rate well? Only every footy fan in the country.

Perhaps the most prominent voice of protest was that of TV personality and Souths fan Andrew Denton. On his TV show *Live and Sweaty* he announced the 'Free the 33' campaign, a reference to the roughly 33 minutes of league that was not being televised. On that show, he put Nine on trial for 'murdering rugby league' and a phone-in poll drew in 5000 calls with a verdict of 'guilty'.

A later stunt saw him kicked out of Nine's head office for entering with a megaphone and demanding to speak to managing director David Leckie and programming director Ross Plapp.

As part of the campaign ABC shops distributed postcards that people could send to Plapp asking him to move the Sunday news to 5.30 pm to allow 90-minutes of league.

'That way you get your advertising revenue and we get a full game,' the postcard said.

'I will continue to watch your league broadcast because – as you well know – there is no other option. However, as a mark of protest, I will no longer watch your 6 pm Sunday news until you have done the right thing and given us back the missing 33 minutes.'

While there was a dose of humour in the campaign, Denton said there was a serious side too. With the battle for pay TV licences heating up, having the rights to league was a boon for Nine. If they got a licence, they could screen the league – uncut – and be pretty certain footy fans would sign up as subscribers.

Channel Nine stuck to its guns all season and ignored the campaigns, petitions and postcards. Until the 1992 finals series, where it suddenly found the ability to move the Sunday news to 5 pm and have the league run from 5.30 pm to 7.30 pm. The previous night Nine also showed a full two hours of league, from 6.30 pm to 8.30 pm, pushing *Hey, Hey It's Saturday* out of its usual 6.30 pm timeslot.

But league fans needn't have gotten their hopes up that this was some sort of admission that Nine had learned its lesson. The one-hour highlights package returned for the 1993 season and in fact would remain in place for years.

‘I KNEW STRAIGHT AWAY THAT I’D DONE THE WRONG THING.’

26

BETTING ON THE BEST AND FAIREST

The 1994 season was the fag-end of tobacco companies' involvement in rugby league. One of those was ciggie-maker Rothmans, who had its name attached to the award for the game's best player. That year North Sydney's David Fairleigh walked away with the Rothmans Medal, no doubt a time to remember for him.

It was a time to forget for the bookies taking bets on the winner. Many felt there was something on the nose with a number of first-time punters laying out elephant bucks on Fairleigh to win, or even more suspiciously, on a quinella that wrapped up the Norths player with actual runner-up, Manly's Steve Menzies.

The Rothmans Medal was decided by the referees in a 3-2-1 voting system; the best player on the day gets three points, and so on. Those votes then go into a sealed envelope, which is held by a referee's representative before being passed onto the State Electoral Office. At the end of Round 18, the SEO does a count of the votes to work out potential winners and give a video company time to make highlight videos of all the options.

Not until after Round 22 are the last four rounds tallied, giving a final winner.

Fairleigh won on 33 points, with Menzies just behind on 31, with a seven-point gap to third-placed Paul Green. The day after Fairleigh won the medal in early September, Darwin-based agency SportsBet blew the whistle, claiming it had lost up to $50,000. Spokesman Bryan Clark said it looked as though some punters knew the likely results; one first-timer had made suspiciously large bets of $2000, $2350 and $750 since mid-July, which was when Fairleigh and Menzies broke away from the pack.

'A month after the punter made the bets we closed our books,' Clark said. 'Fairleigh went from 14-1 to even money in that period. Menzies went from 10-1 to 4-1 when we closed the books. When we closed up, the punter who we'd never heard of before or since didn't want another bet.'

The following day Gerard Daffy from Centrebet echoed SportsBet's claims, saying they too had been given a bath on Fairleigh betting, paying out $115,000. 'Either someone had a very good crystal ball, or they had a good head-start,' Daffy said. 'Most of the bets were on Fairleigh to win and Menzies each-way. You have to say that the punters had guidance, wouldn't you?'

A punter by the name of Alan Katzmann blabbed that a 'well-known rugby league identity' told him Fairleigh would win the Rothmans. He said he was asked to wait until some others in the know had placed their bets, but decided to plonk his cash down while the odds were good. Katzmann felt the votes had been leaked when he saw a count at the end of Round 12 was almost identical to the Round 11 count he had been told of at the time.

Referees' director Mick Stone said he had heard rumours that Fairleigh had won before the final round, but dismissed them because he had the sealed vote counts for the last few rounds locked up in his office. 'At the end of the day, Rothmans end up with 22 large envelopes, each containing eight small envelopes which have the game, date, name of the referee and his signature on it,' Stone told the *Herald*. 'When I read about the leak, the envelopes for Rounds 19, 20 and 21 hadn't even been opened and Round 22 hadn't been completed.'

League boss John Quayle admitted something had gone 'astray' but they would need evidence to confirm a leak. 'People speculate on so many occasions,' he said, 'but it does look a bit obvious, doesn't it?'

With the votes being the responsibility of the referee, rumours started flying that maybe one of the men in the middle was involved in the leak. That was something that didn't sit at all well with leading referee Greg McCallum, who made it seem like the voting was a chore the refs wanted to get over with as quickly as possible.

'It's the most ridiculous thing I've ever heard in my life,' he said. 'I fill the forms out because I have to and I leave it at that and I know the other referees have a similar attitude. It's just a job we're asked to do by the league.'

The controversy whipped up by claims of a leak saw the big winners reluctant to collect on their bets. Days after the medal ceremony, none of the first-time punters with Centrebet or SportsBet had called to arrange for payment; the overall winnings were more than $100,000. 'With all the furore of the Rothmans

Medal, it appears to have sent them into hiding,' Daffy said. 'I think they will have a few sleepless nights over this, then wait until it dies down and then come forward to collect.'

In the end, the origins of any leak (or even if there was one) remained unclear. The NSW Police investigated and could find no evidence of fraud surrounding the Rothmans Medal. Still, the league and Rothmans made some changes; most notable was the decision not to count votes until the end of the final round, rather than at the end of Rounds 6, 12, 18 and 22. As for the betting agencies, they'd claimed to have had enough of the Rothmans Medal and wouldn't be taking bets again. But they changed their minds when they heard of these new measures.

With the ban on ciggie advertising killing off the Rothmans Medal, it was replaced by the Dally Ms, which would, in time, have their own betting scandal. In 2019, Storm coach Craig Bellamy was considered an outsider to win coach of the year and had been priced at $3 or $4 on 13 September. That was the day all the votes had been counted by StatEdge, the tech company managing the awards, and then passed onto the NRL.

Oddly enough, less than an hour after StatEdge sent the results, police alleged money started to flow in for Bellamy to win. It wasn't any surprise really – the people doing the betting were StatEdge owner Joshua Wilson and director Ben Trevisiol, along with some of their friends.

Trevisiol had leaked to Wilson that Bellamy was going to win. Then Wilson passed on the info to some mates while out at the pub that night. Wilson put on two bets, winning $1975. His friends at the pub got into the action and placed their own bets. Trevisiol didn't miss out either, picking up $950 from the bets he laid right up until the agencies closed the books.

The NRL noted the sudden rush of money for Bellamy but didn't need to launch their own investigation; Wilson owned up to the league's integrity commission not long after the Dally M ceremony. 'When you do the wrong thing, you've just got to put your hand up and own it,' Wilson said after he copped an 18-month good behaviour bond. 'I knew straight away that I'd done the wrong thing. When you do something wrong it's how you bounce back that's the most important thing.'

Trevisiol, whose actions were branded as 'just really stupid', also got an 18-month good behaviour bond. A month after the May 2020 court cases, the NRL decided to ban betting on that year's Dally Ms. As it turned out, that was a very good decision. More than three hours before the player of the year award was announced at the ceremony, the *Telegraph* published a story on its website that identified Canberra's Jack Wighton as the winner. Some journos ae given the results ahead of time so as to get stories ready, on the condition they only run after any announcements have been made.

Had betting on that year's Dally Ms been allowed, there would surely have been a huge flood of people putting some cash on Wighton to win.

‘EVERY HIT HURTS,’ HE SAID. ‘I THINK RUGBY LEAGUE PLAYERS COULD WEAR A LITTLE MORE PADDING.’

27

THE AMERICAN LEAGUE

Every now and then, an American turns up on Australian shores keen to try their hand at rugby league. Possibly the first was Al Kirkland, who had visited as part of the American All-Stars side in 1953. To confuse matters, there were actually two Al Kirklands in the All-Stars – Alfred Kirkland and Alvin Kirkland. The former played lock while the latter impressed the local media as a centre. He scored 11 tries on the Australian leg of the tour, including four in the visitors' win over Monaro-Southern Division and three in their 62-41 loss to NSW.

In the mid-1950s, Parramatta – who had been in the comp for a decade – wasn't setting the competition on fire. In 1956, the club looked to the US for a circuit breaker and invited Alvin Kirkland back to Australia. He trained with the reserve-grade squad but he was good enough to be named in the Round 1 team to take on Balmain. He ended up playing in all 18 games that season, playing wing and centre before finishing up the losing season, where they won just four games, at five-eighth. Kirkland left at the end of the 1956 season and headed off to England, where he played for Leeds.

It would be 1977 before another American played first-grade rugby league. That was the year NFL player Manfred Moore flew over to play half a season at Newtown. Moore had spent two seasons with the San Francisco 49ers before being drafted by the Tampa Bay Buccaneers in 1976. In an incredible stroke of luck, he was dropped by the 13-0 Bucs, only to be picked by the Oakland Raiders just before the play-offs. The Raiders won it all that year, and Moore became a Super Bowl winner.

And then he headed to Newtown, arriving on a flight in late February with Jack Gibson. Newtown's secretary Frank Farrington had gone to the US with Gibson when he was Newtown coach in 1972 and had been entertaining the idea of bringing over an American player ever since.

Farrington had kept in touch with the 49ers to see if there was a player that would suit league. Former San Francisco coach Dick Nolan thought of Moore and gave him a call. 'I thought, "Hey, great I can play football in the United States, sure I can go and play football in Australia",' Moore said years later. 'Then Dick stopped me and said: "No, no, no, no. It's rugby".'

'I had played rugby one time in college between football seasons, so I didn't really hesitate.'

The Newtown staff showed him a few things, he watched some games on film and managed to find himself in the team for Round 1 against Wests a month later. In a moment from a Hollywood script, he scored the first try – outjumping Wests' fullback John Dorahy to score in the 28th minute. He started out in the centre but moved to the wing. 'Give me a couple of games to get fit and used to rugby league and I think I'll improve a whole lot,' he said. The NFL player was also asked how tough league was. 'Every hit hurts,' he said. 'I think rugby league players could wear a little more padding.'

Newtown won that first match 17-10, but Moore would never again be on a winning Jets team. The team didn't win another game until the final-round clash against Souths, by which time Moore was long gone.

But while he was in town, Moore was a bit of a drawcard for Newtown – as well as a novelty act. In the second-round clash against Penrith, Moore was told to throw two footballs over the stand – NFL style. Moore later said Farrington blindsided him, coming up with the balls at half-time and telling him what he had to do. That's doubtful, given the stunt was promoted in the papers in the days before the game.

It was a big ask for Moore, partially because Farrington could not remember anyone even kicking a ball over the stand.

'The last person I remember who tried to kick one over was Tommy Kirk some years ago and he failed after hitting the roof,' he said of a player who last played for the club in 1946.

'However, Manfred is confident that his American way of throwing will enable him to succeed. If he fails, the balls will go into the crowd for the kids.'

With the crowd watching, Moore couldn't back down, so he grabbed the first ball from Farrington.

'I backed up a little bit like a javelin thrower, and then threw it,' he said. 'It went up and up and then, all of a sudden, it went down … into the stand. I was so embarrassed.

'It was like I was an embarrassment to my country, to African Americans, my family and the NFL football teams I'd played on. Then Frank said: "That's OK, mate", and he tossed me the second ball.

'I put my head down and said: "Lord, help me!". I backed up again, and I threw it, and that ball took off, it was a perfect spiral and it spiralled up and up and over and out of the stadium and the crowd went crazy.'

Moore's presence also gave some reporters licence to engage in flights of fantasy that league players would soon end up wearing more padding than those in the NFL. In one of those pieces, league medical officer Dr Bill Monaghan said he wasn't in favour of helmets, but thought protective padding was a good idea. 'Anything can happen when two extremely large footballers crash into each other at top speed,' he said.

The same story suggested Newtown would be the first club to start wearing 'American-style gear' – which obviously never happened.

Moore played what ended up being his last game against Cronulla in Round 6. He left the field in the second half with a forehead gash that required stitching.

'I started towards the sideline and they said, "No, you've got to get back in there", Moore remembered. 'I thought, "OK, if I'm going to die I'm going to take someone with me." I went back out and I tackled their star player.

'My head drove into his ribs and he was lying on the ground and … he was in such pain and I felt so bad. I was ready to retire from sports after that.'

While the plan was that he would stay until June, Moore returned home in early May. At the start of the year, Farrington predicted US footballers like Moore were the way of the future. 'I think he will be the start of a hell of a lot of American footballers coming here,' Farrington said. 'There are only 28 top teams in the whole of America; get the players who just miss out, and you'll be getting some pretty good-quality footballers.'

By the end of the season, the club had changed their tune. A *Herald* news report in late 1977 stated the club had seen the Moore experiment as 'a failure' and wouldn't be pursuing any more Americans.

It wasn't until 1999 that the next American made it to the top grade. That was Newcastle's Greg Smith. The common belief among fans is that he knocked on coach Warren Ryan's door, said he played NFL and, next thing he knew, he was in the first-grade side for Round 3. The reality is a little bit different, but also a little stranger.

Ryan had heard of Smith before; the American was in the 1997 US World Sevens team coached by Ryan. Smith said he thought it would be fun to play and said yes, only to later discover he was mistaken in thinking he'd been asked to play Australian rules. In 1998, he signed up with Wests and played a season in their Metropolitan Cup side, winning their Rookie of the Year award.

Ryan took a punt on him for the 1999 season, and felt he went well in the trials. 'Greg Smith showed a lot of ability in defence,' Ryan said after the Knights 52-12 trial loss to Canberra, 'and also did some good things in attack. He also ran well out of dummy half so for a bloke who hasn't played a lot of rugby league, he showed us some good things.'

Those things were good enough to earn Smith a wing spot in the Round 3 match against the Bulldogs. 'I can't wait until Sunday,' Smith said, 'and I just want to get as involved as I can, do whatever it takes to contribute to the team and hopefully score a few tries.'

He didn't score any, but managed to let a few in. The Knights were up 24-4 early in the second half, but Smith spilled the ball twice deep in their own territory. The Dogs got the ball and then scored soon afterwards, running out winners 28-26. He was also criticised for poor passing and missed tackles.

On top of that, there were claims Smith had misrepresented his athletic history in America. On the day of his first-grade debut, *The Sunday Telegraph* claimed Smith had said he played in the NFL as a wide receiver with the Philadelphia Eagles in 1995 and 1996. He allegedly played 18 games in his first season and 16 in his second, and scored six touchdowns.

Indeed the Knights' local paper the *Newcastle Herald* had reported that he played two seasons with the Eagles in the time before his league debut. That same story even quoted Knights forward Bill Peden saying teammates were watching him 'knowing he comes from an NFL background'. However, in fairness to Smith, there don't seem to be any interviews at the time where he is directly quoted as saying he played for two seasons.

Written in a time before the internet was all-encompassing, the reporter from *The Sunday Telegraph* rang Eagles officials and football journalists at the city's leading newspapers – no one had heard of Smith.

'He never played for us,' an Eagles spokesman said. 'I just checked the all-time roster and he is not there. He could have been a triallist. We get plenty of those each season, but there has definitely never been a Greg Smith on our roster.'

Philadelphia reporters checked the club's media guides for 1996 and 1997, only to find Smith wasn't there. When confronted by the paper about the conjecture over his career, he proffered a newspaper clipping that said he had signed a one-year contract in 1995. But he had nothing to show he had played for the Eagles. 'They have changed management over there,' he said when asked why the club had never heard of him, 'that must be the reason. I definitely played with them.'

Immediately afterwards, Ryan rose to Smith's defence, stating the extent of his NFL career was irrelevant. 'He wasn't signed to play here for any reason other than being a rugby league player with a lot of speed and he deserved his run.'

However, Smith's fall from grace with the Knights continued. He had been dropped back to the Knights' First Division side and, in mid-April, he was dropped to the bench for that team. Later in the 1999 season, the Knights sacked Smith.

The one-gamer had threatened legal action against *The Sunday Telegraph* for defamation of character, but no case seems to have gone ahead. Then, for years, the rumours around Smith swirled, until he agreed to a TV interview with Peter Sterling in late 2015.

There he said he had signed a free agent contract with the Eagles in 1995 and was one of the 100-plus athletes fighting to make the 53-man roster. He said he remembered looking at the depth charts for his position and, of the 12 wide receivers trying out, he was number 12. He said he used that as motivation and ended up being one of the 53 chosen. Only to be cut 24 hours later.

Which means he was part of the Eagles team – but only for the briefest of periods. Still, even making an NFL roster for a few days is an achievement. Sterling also asked whether Smith misrepresented his NFL 'career' in Australia. To which Smith replied 'not at all', before going off on a tangent about how he felt people could say whatever they wanted, he just needed to focus on his game and 'go out there and perform to the best of my ability'.

As an answer it's not entirely convincing, especially due to the sharp change of the subject. Still, it may be the truth. But what remains unclear is where the suggestion that he played two seasons with the Eagles came from. The *Newcastle Herald* reported that claim three days before that Round 3 match against Canterbury – so it was going around before *The Sunday Telegraph* story that raised questions. That 'two-year' claim had to have come from *somewhere*. Someone had to have told the local paper that information.

Another head-scratching part of the tale is why the Knights didn't seem to have checked Smith's bona fides with the Eagles. It's something you'd expect in any job interview. Yes, it was in the days before a simple Google search would give you the answers, but a few phone calls would surely have been worth the effort.

One thing is certain – while there are a lot of ex-players with one first-grade game to their name, it's unlikely any of them will ever get more attention, and be more remembered, than Greg Smith.

28

THE MOUTH OF THE MAN

Both coaches said Anthony Mundine's comments didn't influence the scoreline, but we know that has to be crap. You give an opponent ammunition like that and it's a no-brainer that they'll use it as motivation to beat you worse than a red-headed stepchild who just dropped a chocolate Paddle Pop on his new mother's white carpet.

Yes, we're talking about the Storm's infamous 70-10 flogging of the Dragons at the Melbourne Cricket Ground in 2000. Neither team was travelling well at the time. It was Round 5 and the Dragons had only won one of their four games to place them in 13th spot.

People now have this image of the Storm as world-beaters, but they were going even worse. They'd lost their first four games of the season and were in 14th spot – more commonly known as last place. So it was last playing second-last and no one expects anything much when those two meet up.

Both sides were desperate for a win and would happily take inspiration from whatever source was offering some. For the Storm, that source happened to be Mundine – a wannabe

Muhammad Ali who had all the arrogance of the great boxer but none of the humour and charisma that leavened the attitude (but who, oddly, away from the spotlight, was a humble, easygoing guy). The teams were last year's grand finalists and ahead of this rematch, Mundine chose to insult the Storm. 'What do I think of Melbourne Storm, the current premiers? I think they are nothing but pretenders.' In his mind the Dragons were the champions and were heading to Melbourne to prove that to everyone.

Now this flight of fancy of Mundine's ignored the fact the Dragons were ahead 14-0 at half-time in the 1999 grand final. It also ignored the very big fact that a Mundine blunder cost St George Illawarra the chance to put the game to bed. With the second half 10 minutes old and the Dragons up 14-2, Mundine grubbered from the 10-metre line and ended up regathering just a few metres from the try line.

With a defender right in front of him and two teammates unmarked on his left, Mundine went for the line. And the defender knocked the ball loose (in his biography he infuriated many a Dragons fan when he said he did what any confident player would do and he had no regrets).

In the grand final, the Dragons had one hand on the premiership trophy only to let it go. So Mundine's comments were just farcical. Publicly Dragons coach David Waite didn't see anything wrong with what Mundine said, while Storm coach Chris Anderson poured cold water on the idea he would use it to fire up the troops – 'I don't like negative motivation', he said. But you just knew that wasn't true.

The game itself was an ugly mess from a Red V point of view. The Dragons had possession for just 17 minutes of the game – seven of those in the first half. The score was 6-0 after four minutes, 12-0 three minutes later, 18-0 five minutes after that and 42-4 at half-time. St George Illawarra looked like a team that didn't care; *they* looked like the team that were grand final pretenders.

Waite reiterated his claim that Mundine's words didn't spark the slaughter, but his actions suggested otherwise. After the shellacking, Mundine – and the rest of the team – were banned from talking to the media for two weeks. The Dragons five-eighth was spared the axe for the following week's match against the Tigers but he'd end up giving himself the chop just over a month later.

Sidelined with a shoulder injury he sustained against the Roosters in Round 10, Mundine was still expected to turn up on game day. He wasn't in the stands when the Dragons beat Penrith in a Saturday night game in Round 12. The buzz was that he had skipped the country, which was confirmed by his mum on the Sunday and on Monday by a Customs officer at the airport who saw him leave.

But the club tried to play it cool by insisting he wasn't really AWOL; the players had Sunday and Monday off so Mundine wasn't missing at all. Until Tuesday, of course, when he didn't turn up for training. The Mundine shenanigans didn't help his teammates; frustrations boiled over at training with some players saying if it had been anyone else who disappeared the club would have sacked them.

The first Saturday after he left, the Dragons got whipped by the Cowboys 50-4. The next day teammates got even hotter under the collar when they opened up the Sunday papers and saw Mundine's smiling face and read that he didn't run away but rather was just 'chilling out' on the US West Coast. The day after he doubled down on the delusion by appearing on TV saying 'I never run from anything. I face it head-on. I'm a man.'

When he finally stopped running away and came home, the club was itching to sack him. But Mundine beat them to the punch. Turning up late to the leagues club for a meeting, ridiculously sucking on a lollipop, he told them he was quitting to become a boxer. 'From today, I'm no longer part of rugby league,' he said. 'I've retired.'

His former teammates never got an explanation from him about the international shenanigans. But they showed how much of a relief it was to be done with it all; a few days later the Dragons handed out a whooping at WIN Stadium, beating Auckland 54-0.

Winger Amos Roberts scored 22 points on debut, a club record and just a point short of the all-time record held by Andrew Johns. 'I hope this is the end of it and now we can bury the issue,' captain Craig Smith said after the game. 'I took a stance during the whole circus on behalf of a lot of the players who were fairly guarded about what was going on, because I thought we were being left out.'

Come the end of the season the Dragons would be left out again, missing the finals by one win.

29

A BUM RAP

It's not going to surprise anyone that John Hopoate has racked up quite an impressive record of suspension. Over the 13 and a bit seasons he played in the NRL – for Manly, the Northern Eagles and Wests Tigers – he had been suspended for 45 weeks. That's almost the equivalent of two full seasons.

Though, despite what some claim, it doesn't seem Hopoate's 45 weeks is the longest total in league history. To award him that dubious crown, one has to forget Les Boyd and his dramas with the judiciary in the 1970s and '80s. Big Les got a year's suspension for breaking Darryl Brohman's jaw in a State of Origin match and then 15 months for eye-gouging Billy Johnstone in just his third game back. Add the odd week or two he copped here and there and Boyd is way ahead of Hopoate.

Like Boyd, the bulk of Hopoate's time on the sideline stemmed from two separate incidents. There was the 17 weeks he copped for jumping up at Shark Keith Galloway and knocking him out with a forearm to the head. When referee Paul Simpkins sent him off the field, Hopoate was stunned and couldn't believe it was called illegal contact. It was the last game he played in the NRL; the Sea Eagles, the club who had been his home for most of those 13 seasons, had finally realised he was a liability and sacked him.

That 2005 incident was the second-longest suspension in the NRL era. The longest was handed down to the Storm's Danny Williams in 2004 when he got 18 weeks for a vicious king-hit on Tiger Mark O'Neill a year earlier. Williams resented the high tackle O'Neill dished out and so, after the play-the-ball, he walked straight to the Tigers forward – who wasn't even looking at him – and hit him in the jaw with a right. Like Hopoate, it was the last NRL game Williams played.

The other incident that makes up a chunk of Hopoate's 45 weeks was the 12 weeks he was pinged for sticking his fingers in backsides of several Cowboys. In the Round 5, 2001, match at Townsville, Wests Tigers' Hopoate jammed his fingers into the back passages of forwards Peter Jones and Glenn Morrison and centre Paul Bowman. It was during a time when the Tigers didn't need any more headaches. The club was already dealing with the positive drug tests of Craig Field and Kevin McGuinness – for cocaine and ecstasy respectively.

When Hopoate was charged, his case was heard on the same night, which was a nightmare for the Wests Tigers. On top of Hoppa's suspension, Field and McGuinness were out for six months. The only upside for those two was that Hopoate's actions pretty much drew all the attention away from them.

While Cowboys players made on-field complaints, the issue only went to the judiciary after Cowboys officials lodged a written complaint – though they were apparently too embarrassed to write down what he did. Instead they rang judiciary commissioner Jim Hall to describe it verbally.

Tigers coach Terry Lamb was not happy with what was going on, suggesting the NRL was trying to rub Hoppa out of the game. 'Hopoate's not a bad boy but the league, or the media, are painting him that way,' the coach said of a player who just a year earlier had been charged with 10 counts of contrary conduct from the one match.

He also suggested that what Hopoate did wasn't really that bad. 'He's just done a little niggling something in the game,' Lamb said. 'He hasn't hurt a bloke, for Christ's sake, and they want to cite him for it. We've all played the game of footy.

'Over the years I've had blokes grab the family jewels, blokes gouge me, blokes pull my hair just to get me off my game. I didn't complain about that. I know it's part of the game. You've just got to handle it.'

Commissioner Hall didn't agree, saying that 'in my 45 years involvement in rugby league I've never come across a more disgusting allegation'. Hopoate's defence amounted to little more than claims he was trying to give opponents a wedgie, which even a single viewing of the match footage would show was clearly not the case.

While the finger-poking in that game was already set to become the thing most people thought of when they heard the name 'John Hopoate', it got a lot worse. Other players came out of the woodwork and claimed he did it to them as well. Brisbane players Wendell Sailor and Michael De Vere said he'd done the same thing to them a few weeks earlier. St George Illawarra player Craig Smith said he'd received the Hoppa treatment earlier that season too. One unnamed player claimed it happened the previous season as well. That player was suspended for punching Hoppa in response but, as he pleaded guilty, he didn't have to front the tribunal and air that information.

Hopoate released the obligatory apology, where he said he was planning to see a counsellor to learn how to become a better person. 'I was just trying to niggle the opposition and gain an advantage,' he said. 'It was stupid. I don't know why I have these brain explosions … I'm going to have to get counselling. I've had about two hours sleep over the past three days. It's killing me at night. I just keep going over and over it in my mind … why.'

Part of the reason he did it, it was later revealed, was so his teammates would have something to laugh at while doing video sessions later in the week. That got Lamb in hot water when the club found out he and players laughed when they watched footage of Hopoate doing it to Craig Smith. If Lamb had been responsible enough to tell Hopoate to quit it there and then, the Wests Tigers could have avoided a very public embarrassment.

'We watched the incident involving Smith and we all had a bit of a laugh,' Lamb said. 'We thought it was okay because Hoppa is good mates with Craig. Looking back at what I know, we would have taken action. I don't feel guilty, though, because I didn't know about all the other incidents. Regardless of everything, I'll go into the board meeting and more than likely back Hoppa.'

That meeting was to decide Hoppa's future at the club – as well as those of Field and McGuinness. Those two were fined a part of their contract for every match they were suspended, which amounted to more than $200,000 each, and had to submit to weekly drug tests for the next six months. Hopoate ended up resigning before the club could sack him.

ABOVE South Sydney winger Terry Fahey gets away from Canterbury's Mark Hughes during the first League-A-Thon at the Sydney Cricket Ground in April 1977.

BELOW Newtown players Phil Sigsworth, Ken Wilson and Steve Bowden look disconsolate after playing a scoreless draw against Canterbury in 1982.

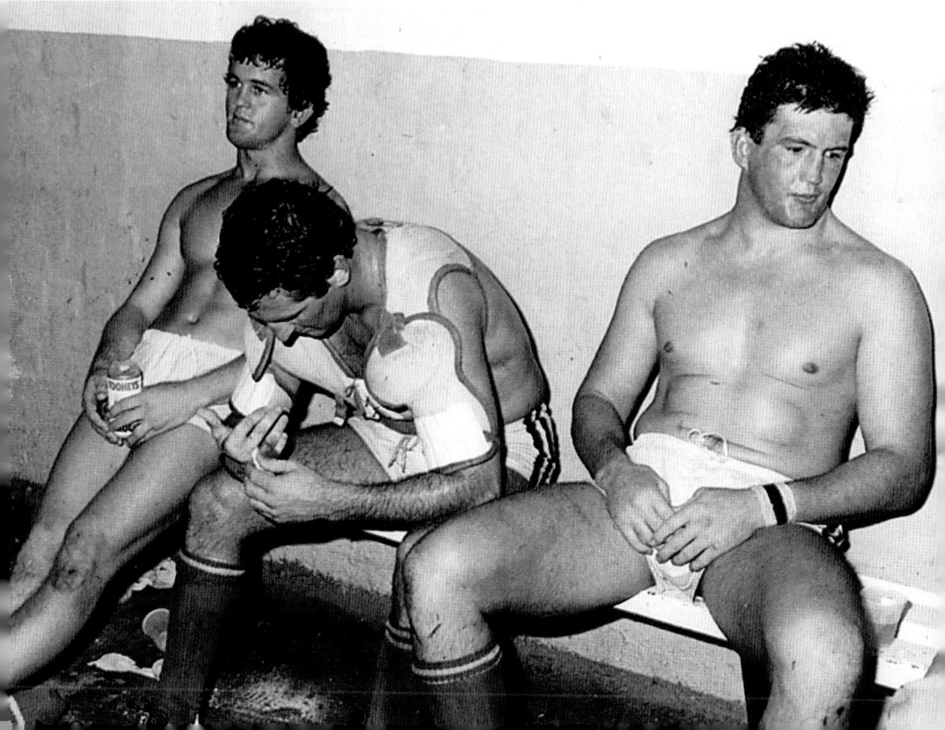

ABOVE Jack Gibson sporting his iconic kangaroo fur coat in the sheds after a match in 1981. There is still some debate around what actually happened to that jacket.

BELOW Gibson talking to the first grade Eels side in the bus that was often used while their home ground facilities were upgraded.

ABOVE Arriving in the competition in 1982 it took Illawarra several years before the local steelworks owner BHP became their main sponsor. The club had picked the Steelers name to try and entice them.

LEFT Mike Eden joined the new Gold Coast club in 1988. The club first played under the Giants moniker, then Seagulls, Gladiators and finally Chargers.

ABOVE Super League saw the creation of several short-lived clubs, including the Adelaide Rams (red and blue) and the much-disliked Hunter Mariners (blue and yellow).

BELOW Mark O'Meley loved Deep Heat so much he would rub it into his shaved head to motivate himself before a game.

ABOVE Former PM John Howard with a sod of turf from Birchgrove Oval where the first match in the Sydney rugby league competition was played in 1908. The sod was destined for a commemorative time capsule.

BELOW The corner post's role has changed over the years. Here Cronulla's cover defence swamps Roosters' Mitchell Aubusson for a no try at Shark Park in 2008.

ABOVE The Manly Sea Eagles and South Sydney Rabbitohs mascots get into a fight at Brookvale Oval in 2008.

ABOVE Tigers star Benji Marshall was one of a number of players hoodwinked by the useless Power Balance wristband.

BELOW It's become a tradition for the captains of the teams in the NRL finals to gather for a 'photo call'. Here the skippers of the 2018 finalists pose in front of a large version of the iconic 'Gladiators' premiership trophy.

ABOVE The Dragons' Jason Nightingale runs the ball under an orange sunset during the St George-Illawarra Dragons v Cronulla Sharks NRL match at Kogarah in Sydney in 2015.

'His last words were, "I'm going off to church now, I'll pray for the team and wish them good luck",' chairman John Chalk said. 'I just think he's been pushed that far and he was extremely emotional yesterday and this morning. He was worried about his family's situation and he was worried about his church situation and his cultural background is obviously a problem for him.'

Lamb also came under the focus of the club's investigation for not acting earlier. He escaped with a slap on the wrist and went on to coach the Tigers for another season. As for Hopoate, many felt his NRL career was over so it came as a surprise that the newly formed Northern Eagles signed him up.

Club chairman Dick Harris went down to the sheds after a Round 16 win over Penrith at Brookvale to tell the team Hopoate was coming. 'At best, I expected a stunned silence, followed by a lot of awkward questions after I asked them to make John welcome,' he said. 'Instead, the players clapped. I was very pleasantly surprised.'

His first game after serving the suspension was in the Manly First Division side playing the Dragons on 14 July. The following week he was a surprise inclusion in the top grade against the Sharks and then was in the side seven days later to face the Tigers, who pummelled the Northern Eagles 38-6.

It would be a few years before Hoppa became a headache for his new team. In 2003 he breached his contract by playing in a fifth-grade union match – under a fake name so he wouldn't get caught. But he was and the club fined him $5000. The following season he was outed for nine weeks for threatening interchange official Darren Alchin after a 40-point loss to Parramatta.

Both Alchin and fellow official Steve Chiddy said Hopoate had started things, goading Chiddy by saying: 'You're just a bloody touch judge'. When Alchin intervened, telling Hopoate to 'shut it', the winger stepped forward and said, 'Don't tell me to shut up – I'll knock you out, you faggot'.

Hopoate said he had not recognised Alchin's uniform as that of a league official, suggesting he felt his crime was not what he said, but who he said it to. Incidentally, he was also cited for fighting in that same match.

Hopoate didn't return until Round 1 the following season, but only managed to hold it together for two games before cracking Galloway with an elbow and the club realising he wasn't worth hanging onto any more.

As a postscript, a 2018 incident conclusively showed Hopoate didn't understand where to draw the line. Despite being under a 10-year ban from rugby league after punching players in a Grade A match, Hopoate was a controversial late inclusion for a Legends of League charity event featuring ex-players from a range of clubs.

He was allowed to take part because the match was not overseen by the NSWRL and therefore not subject to the ban. But still, the organisers should have known better than to allow a banned player to take the field.

Playing for a Manly side against a team of former Newcastle players, Hopoate took to the field wearing a rubber glove on his left hand. Amazingly no officials or organisers told him to take it off. And so, not long into the match he pretended to stick a few gloved fingers into an opponent's backside.

Charming.

30

HEADGEAR

In late 2020 NRL.com carried out a poll to find the best headgear-wearing player of the last 30 years. There were some illustrious names on that list – Steve Menzies, Steve Renouf and Daryl Harrigan – as well as Jamie Soward, Kalyn Ponga, Mark Carroll and Matt Sing.

But as far as those who voted in the poll were concerned, there was only ever going to be one winner – Johnathan Thurston. The former Cowboys captain and premiership winner scored half of the 13,787 votes cast. His nearest rival was Menzies with 23 per cent of the vote. The results may have injured the pride of 'Spud' Carroll, who didn't get a single vote.

Throughout his career, headgear became synonymous with Thurston – he even championed the colour-coded style, ensuring his headgear was always in team colours.

He hadn't always worn the protective padding on his noggin – and it wasn't part of some deal his mum made him agree to before he could play footy as a kid. According to his autobiography, headgear didn't become an option until he turned 17, and the coach of the local A-Grade team thought Thurston good enough to step up and play against grown men.

The teen figured he'd have a go but quickly regretted his decision after the first training run. 'My new teammates were all battle-hardened giants, behemoths with beards and bulging biceps ... shit I'm going to get myself killed.'

So the next day he went down to the local sports store and asked to be pointed in the direction of the headgear. 'Being so young, and so small, I wanted to protect myself as much as possible. I wasn't even 70 kilograms yet. So I got myself my very first headgear and I have worn one in every match since.'

What really solidified the idea of headgear with Thurston was his habit of giving it away matches. It's a habit he reckoned started in 2016 when a kid in the crowd yelled to him, 'Hey, JT, give us your headgear'. Thurston took it off and handed it to the kid – and the smile he got in return changed everything.

The next day Thurston was on the phone to sponsor Madison Sports asking for more headgear – one for every remaining match that season. Obviously, the sponsor wanted to know what he was going to do with all of them. 'I gave one away to a kid at the game last night and you should have seen the look on his face. I want to make a kid smile like that every week.'

Soon after that call, a box of fresh headgear arrived at his place. Then Thurston asked for twice as much – figuring he could give one away at half-time and a second at full time. 'I can make two kids happy instead of one,' he told the sponsor. JT soon got what he asked for.

Since that time, Thurston has given away more than $40,000 worth of headgear – which is more than his sponsorship with Madison is worth. Not that Madison Sports' director Brian

Carmody cares. 'There's a cost to us associated with it,' he told *The Sunday Telegraph*, 'which is over and above the endorsement fee we pay him, but I think it's a wonderful thing for the game and for Johnathan to do.'

Though it did backfire after a match against Parramatta. At the end of the game, Thurston zeroed in on a kid in the front row wearing an Eels jersey. There was an adult either side of the kid and both went to grab the headgear, only for Thurston to pull it away. He actually had several goes at trying to get it to the kid before the adult arms stopped trying to grab it.

Thurston then turned his back on the kid, and so didn't see what happened next; the kid turned it over in his hand and then, with a look of disgust on his face, dropped it over the fence and back onto the field.

Turns out it wasn't some display of dislike directed at the Cowboys captain. The kid's dad got in touch with the club to explain he was afraid of germs and so freaked out when Thurston put his dirty, sweaty headgear into his hand. The following week, the Cowboys played Penrith and Thurston tracked down the kid while in western Sydney to hand him a brand spanking new – and clean – jersey.

While the headgear has certainly been good for Thurston's image, it might not have done all that much for his health. Thurston believes it had saved him from serious injury, but the medical fraternity says there are no significant benefits to wearing headgear.

In a 2012 match against the Dragons, Thurston was hit in the jaw with an elbow from the Red V's Matt Prior. He left the field dazed but was convinced things would have been worse without his signature headgear.

'Where he got me, if I wasn't wearing the headgear I think I could have had a broken cheekbone or a broken jaw or something like that,' he told *The Courier-Mail*. 'So I'm very glad I wear the headgear.'

That same season he was also hit with a shoulder charge by Shark Ben Pomeroy. After the game, Cowboys coach Neil Henry said he was initially worried about Thurston's health 'but he wears headgear'.

That comment prompted NRL chief medical officer Ron Muratore to contact the *Herald* to explain the limitations of headgear. 'The only thing headgear protects you from is lacerations around the scalp and face,' he said. 'That is really the only thing. For the concussion, it does nothing because concussion is the brain moving inside the skull and there is no way you can stop that.

'I don't know how we can get the message through to people and educate them that headgear makes no difference, and in fact if you give it to kids it often gives them a false sense of security.'

31

THE C WORD

Whether it's on the knee, wrist, shoulders, ankles or some other body part, players rely on strapping for a varied array of reasons. Sometimes, it's to help them get on the field with a niggle, sometimes it's to stop an injury from getting worse. Other times it can be a confidence thing; the feeling of tape wrapped around a limb can make a player more willing to put that limb to the test in a tackle or hit-up. And sometimes, it can be a blame-shifter; a player prone to dropping a ball or two might get some strapping near his hands so, when he next spills the pill, he can use that strapping as an excuse.

Players can also use it as a billboard of sorts to advertise their thoughts. Maybe they scrawl their kids' names on it or a few words to God or even some generic motivational words. Every now and then, a player's handiwork can get them into trouble.

One of those was forward Matt Lodge in 2014 – the year before he ran amok in a New York hotel and scared the life out of some German tourists. In 2014, Lodge was a part of the Melbourne Storm under 20s team playing in the Toyota Cup. He had been going well enough to get picked for NSW in the under 20s State of Origin, meeting up with the Maroons at Penrith Stadium in May.

He got in some strife during a brawl in the first half, where he was sin binned after throwing two right-hand jabs over his teammates to clock a Queenslander in the side of the head. The judiciary gave him a one-week ban for the punches.

And a two-week ban for his creativity with a black texta. Television cameras clearly picked up the writing on Lodge's wrist strapping, which included the dreaded C word. Of course there was umbrage on social media – though there couldn't have been heaps of it because the audience for under 20s rep games can't be huge.

The purpose of writing that word on his wrist is unclear. Was it some peculiar sort of self-abuse designed to make himself angry and attack the opposition? Was it a reminder to use that word to insult a rival on the field? Or was it just something that made the young footballer giggle in the sheds before the game? The latter seems most likely. At any rate, Lodge managed to get out of the sheds and onto the field without any NSW team officials noticing his penmanship. By the time he was sin binned, word had gotten around about it and the officials told him to remove it.

The very same word got New Zealand Warriors prop Kane Evans in trouble in 2021 during a match against the Panthers. Coincidentally, Lodge was playing for the Warriors at the time and apparently didn't suggest to Evans this wasn't his brightest idea.

The odd thing about the Evans incident is that he didn't get on the field in that game. He was the 18th man for the Warriors but was never called on. But the TV cameras focused on him sitting on the sideline, getting a full view of the words 'fold some c..t' scrawled on his wrist strapping.

'If Evans is that much of an imbecile,' noted ABC *Grandstand* commentator Andrew Moore, 'he should be suspended before he takes the field.' Evans wasn't suspended but he was fined $5000 by the NRL, which also had to tell the other players that writing rude words on strapping was not the best idea they could have.

'Anything that you put on your playing equipment in terms of writing,' said NRL's head of football Graham Annesley, 'or anything that you may carry attached to your equipment that is considered to be non-standard in any way, you can't expect that it won't be picked up.

'There are cameras all over the venue. It's all in high-definition, it's very easy to pick these things up.'

Perhaps the most controversial bit of writing on strapping didn't have a single swear word. In fact it didn't have any words at all – just three letters written to support a convicted killer.

In 2016 Sharks prop Andrew Fifita had taken to the field at least six times with the initials FKL in large black texta on his forearm strapping. Apparently it took that long for someone to wonder what it stood for.

The letters stood for 'For Kieran Loveridge,' a man who killed Thomas Kelly with a single punch to the head while the former was leaving a nightclub on the night of July 7, 2012. Kelly fell backwards onto the footpath, causing a fatal fracture to his skull in what was a completely random assault. Loveridge fronted court and was sentenced to 10 years and two months in jail.

Fifita was childhood friends with Loveridge and in 2016 decided to send him a message via his wrist strapping.

The Sharks prop got away with it for weeks until the alarm was raised late in the season after police issued him with a notice for consorting with criminals after repeated visits to Loveridge in Cessnock jail.

The notice was issued by Task Force Raptor, set up to tackle outlaw motorcycle gangs. While in jail, Loveridge was believed to have developed links to the Lone Wolf bikie gang.

'The player was visited by members of the NSW Police earlier in the week and put on notice that he cease any further contact with Loveridge based on facts the police had in relation to the latter's links to other criminal elements,' the club said in a statement.

'In talking with the police, while emphasising that no allegations of unlawful behaviour have been levelled against Andrew, they confirm that they have issued a verbal warning because they are concerned about the potential for organised crime to infiltrate sport through criminal elements and for NRL players to be unwittingly drawn into that web.'

The NRL then conducted its own investigations, from which arose the initials FKL. His coach Shane Flanagan said it wasn't possible for a club to keep track of everything players wrote on tape. 'Players usually have crosses for religious beliefs,' he said, 'most halves have special plays on there and I know Gal [Paul Gallen] had a sick kid's name who passed away recently written on his arm.'

Fifita opened up about the issue in September, just after the Sharks qualified for the grand final. 'From my belief, and everyone knows the story of my friendship, and my family know what it meant,' he said. 'I have no regrets about that. I know it was wrong from a public's [perspective] looking inside. I couldn't speak about it [at the time]. I'm pretty positive and upbeat about it.'

It seemed in contradiction to his statement released by the Sharks a few weeks earlier, where he did in fact express regret. 'I fully understand and accept the seriousness of the crime committed by Loveridge, the devastating impact it has had on the Kelly family and the need for Loveridge to serve his time,' he said in the statement.

'I want to extend my sincere apologies to the Kelly family for any distress caused to them by having this tragic matter back in the media.'

In December, a few months after Fifita played in the Sharks' drought-breaking premiership win, the NRL announced it would fine him $20,000 and issued a warning that any further breaches of the league's code of conduct would lead to his contract being deregistered.

After the fine was levied, Fifita said he had only been trying to lift a friend's spirits. 'I was helping out a mate,' he said. 'That's all that matters. He wasn't doing too well at the time. I gave him the boost that he really needs.'

IT SEEMS VAUGHAN STARTED TEXTING A FEW TEAMMATES SAYING 'DUDES, BEERS AND SNAGS AT MINE 2MORO, YO!'

32

THE SEASON-ENDING BBQ

It always seemed that the record for the most players suspended from a single incident would forever be held by the 1917 Glebe side. Fourteen of their players were suspended after they boycotted a match in protest at the league's decision to move it to a different ground.

But the Dragons team of 2021 gave that record an almighty shake, falling just one player shy of equalling the record. The St George Illawarra players' transgression was the now-infamous barbeque at prop Paul Vaughan's house. Held in violation of the COVID lockdown rules in place at the time, the barbeque torched the Dragons' season.

They were sitting in seventh spot having just beaten the Warriors 19-18 and looking like they might make the finals for the first time since 2018. But the wheels fell off when the party house was busted by police and Dragons players scattered. After that moment, St George Illawarra didn't win another game, dropping eight straight as though they were chasing the wooden spoon. They finished the season in 11th place, though there was a bit of a logjam at the bottom of the NRL ladder that season.

The party had its origins in a player's suggestion (it wasn't Vaughan, by the way) after the golden point win over the Warriors that the club hold a 'bonding session' at WIN Stadium the following night. Officials said no because of the difficulties in getting inebriated players home to all points of the compass afterwards without breaching COVID rules. Under the NRL biosecurity bubble rules, players were not allowed to use public transport or catch an Uber or a taxi.

With that off the table, it seems Vaughan started texting a few teammates saying 'Dudes, beers and snags at mine 2moro, yo!' (or something like that). Dragons' Origin stars and senior players Ben Hunt, Tariq Sims and Andrew McCullough didn't get the SMS, most likely because if they did they'd have told their teammates just how stupid the whole idea was.

Herald writer Andrew Webster wondered just what the hell the players were celebrating. The win against the Warriors hadn't been spectacular. Nor had their season to date with eight wins and eight losses. Players like Corey Norman were off-contract at the end of the year and unlikely to get another one.

Or maybe things were so bad at the Dragons the players saw fit to celebrate the bye. 'Mediocrity and entitlement have been the standard at St George Illawarra for so long, from the board down, that the club no longer understands what success looks like,' wrote Webster, a Dragons fan.

'While there are conflicting reports about what actually went down at Vaughany's barbie, there's one indisputable part of this story that shines a light on the attitude of some of their players.'

That part was when coach Anthony Griffin and football GM Ben Haran told the players not to get on the turps – but they ignored them and did it anyway.

'It demonstrated something more than a lack of respect for Griffin and Haran. It was straight-out betrayal.'

And so on the Saturday night, with 13 players in Vaughan's Shellharbour house (and most likely other people as well), neighbours called police and said there was a party going on. They knew people in Shellharbour weren't allowed to be having parties and if these footy players were being so obvious about it (they started turning up from 3 pm carrying slabs of beer) they deserved to get caught.

When the police arrived, neighbours saw people coming out of the doors and windows and bolting. These included hot and cold (but mainly cold) five-eighth Corey Norman, who made the cops' job that little bit easier by leaving his wallet with ID in it on the barbecue.

Several people claimed pint-sized speedster Matt Dufty bolted the five kilometres to his own home. Dufty denied that, but he had to have left the place on foot because his car was parked out the front of Vaughan's house.

The most eye-opening presence at the party was that of Jack de Belin, who had just returned to playing a few weeks earlier after rape charges were dropped. The club had stood by him when the league rules forced him to stand down in early 2019. They even paid him while he couldn't play. And instead of thinking, 'You know, I really should keep my nose clean and stay home. Maybe play with my kids', he went to a party.

When the cops came, he hid under a bed while teammates tried to keep his attendance a secret. Then he told the club and the league that he was only in the area because he was walking his dog. There was also the claim that he just dropped off a case of beer and left.

'Obviously Jack's not proud of what happened over the last couple of days,' coach Anthony Griffin said, suggesting something that really wasn't very obvious at all. 'He now needs to perform and repay what the board and the rest of the club have given him.'

The 13 players at the party (let's list them – Vaughan, de Belin, Dufty, Norman, Zac Lomax, Jack Bird, Blake Lawrie, Josh Kerr, Daniel Alvaro, Josh McGuire, Tyrell Fuimaono, Kaide Ellis and Gerard Beale) all copped a $1000 infringement notice from the cops. But that was only the start of the pummelling their hip pocket nerves got.

The NRL were understandably irate about the party; it had negotiated agreements with various state governments so the competition could go ahead, and these Red V clowns had put that in jeopardy. 'I am extremely disappointed, frustrated and to be honest, I am gutted,' said NRL CEO Andrew Abdo. 'There is so much at stake and there are so many people adhering to very, very strict protocols to keep the competition safe and to keep the community safe and to keep the competition going.'

The NRL suspended party-thrower Vaughan for eight weeks and fined him $50,000. The remaining 12 players all received a one-match ban and fines ranging from $50,000 for Norman and $42,000 for de Belin down to $2000 for Beale. All-up, the suspensions totalled 20 weeks but, to avoid the Dragons' having to field a reserve-grade side in their next match, the NRL allowed the club to stagger the suspensions over four weeks.

Abdo said the punishments reflected the seriousness of the players' actions and the fact that some of them withheld information from the NRL's integrity unit. 'On the information we have, the players understood the protocols and deliberately chose to ignore them,' he said.

Dragons CEO Ryan Webb was furious, saying the players' actions were 'infuriating'. The club also fined the players, holding out the harshest punishment for Vaughan – tearing up his $800,000 a year contract. The reason was 'three strikes and you're out'. Vaughan had breached the biosecurity bubble the year before by going to a café and the other strike was a previously unknown instance of sexting, where he sent some dirty pics to a woman two years earlier. Sacking Vaughan had an upside for the club; it ended concerns the forward – whose performances had been subpar – would trigger a contract option for 2022.

'It wasn't an easy decision by any means,' Webb said. 'Paul took the news as you would expect, he took it quite hard. He was probably quite shocked by the news.' He was likely even more shocked once he realised how much money he was going to lose because of a stupid idea to have a party.

'My actions were stupid, unexplainable and irresponsible,' Vaughan said on social media. 'The events that took place on the weekend were thoughtless and disrespectful to not only the game that I love, but to all of the sponsors, members and fans as well as the broader community. The reality is I should have known better and I am truly sorry.'

The rest of the players were also forced into public apologies. Some spent a weekend phoning angry club members to apologise, some took to social media, while others had to front the microphones and voice recorders of the media pack. One of those was Josh McGuire, who gave a refreshingly honest explanation of why they did it.

'We did understand [the rules] and can't sit here and say we didn't understand. We were in Shellharbour, a long way from everything that was happening. The decision of going to the barbecue everyone made, and at the end of the day we didn't think it would be a drama and we wouldn't get caught.'

Ah yes, 'we wouldn't get caught' – the reason so many of us do stupid things. Unlike Vaughan's statement, McGuire knew his actions were entirely explainable.

On the talk of some players running when the police arrived, he said they were scared. 'They were scared of the repercussions and what would happen. It was a flight-or-fight kind of thing. A few of us stood there and talked to police. A few boys didn't want to hang around.'

The round of mea culpas should have been the end of the matter – aside from the month of suspensions, that is. But there was another wrinkle for the party posse. The club called on each of them to sign a sworn statement that there was no one else at the barbecue. The reasoning was sound; the club wanted to know if there had been people outside the bubble present.

Players would not be allowed to return to training or matches until they signed.

Lomax and Alvaro both refused to sign the document, concerned about any legal implications. It was a move that obviously raised questions about whether the players had been totally forthcoming about who was there. The stance became even more problematic when the league had to move the competition – and all the players – to Queensland. Ultimately the pair ended up being allowed into Queensland – and the competition – without signing.

Amazingly, the Dragons weren't alone when it came to COVID stupidity. A few weeks earlier NSW Blues debutante – and married father of two – Apisai Koroisau twice snuck a woman into the team hotels in two separate states. 'I made the choice to do the wrong thing and my actions have brought shame and embarrassment to many people, especially my wife and children. I will be forever sorry,' he said in a prepared statement that sounded all too familiar.

Koroisau copped a two-week suspension and a $35,000 fine – the league noting the offence had occurred prior to the Dragons barbecue blowing up.

The very same week, Queensland rep Jai Arrow was suspended for two games and fined $35,000 for sneaking a woman into the Maroons hotel on the Gold Coast.

'I regret everything about it. I have massive regrets and I'm not proud of what I did,' Arrow later told the *Herald*. 'It's hard to talk about. I haven't spoken about it since then.

'I knew what I was doing [at the time] was wrong, absolutely I did. I've suffered plenty of punishment as a result. It was a dumb decision to make. I've apologised to everyone I've hurt. I lost a lot. It hurts.'

In August Sharks player Josh Dugan was charged by police with a breach of COVID rules after being caught trying to drive to Lithgow. They had been pulled over twice, offering the excuses they were visiting a friend or that they were heading to Lithgow to feed their animals. It had been his second breach after having gone out to a restaurant two months earlier. Not long afterwards, the Sharks chose to sack Dugan, who then retired from footy.

33

GIMMICKS

For decades now, footballers have been keen on gimmicks. Whether it's something that looks good or perhaps they're convinced it gives them an edge, they'll go for it. But, for the most part, they fit the dictionary definition of a gimmick – something designed to grab the attention rather than actually doing anything.

For instance, the magic sponge is a gimmick, only we didn't realise it at the time. Hard to believe these days, but in the 1970s, when a player went down injured, a trainer sporting a spiffy matching tracksuit would run onto the field with a bucket and the magic sponge. The sponge would get soaked and then pressed down on the back of the player's neck. Less than a minute would pass before he was up on his feet and playing again. It's pretty safe to say, exactly the same thing would have happened if the trainer had stayed on the sideline.

An infamous instance of a gimmick from the past is Graeme Langlands' white boots from the 1975 grand final. Back then you had two choices in colours when it came to footy boots – black or nothing. But ex-Kangaroo teammate and friend Ken Irvine was working for Adidas and offered the St George fullback a pair of white boots. Langlands decided to wear them in the grand final against the Roosters.

As history recorded, the Dragons got smacked 38-0 – the biggest grand final defeat until 2008 when Manly tore the Storm to shreds 40-0. But it wasn't the white boots that were the problem for Langlands; he'd gotten a painkilling injection in his groin that deadened his leg. He couldn't run, he couldn't kick. Still at half-time the Dragons were only 5-0 down. If Langlands didn't go on for the second half, St George were in with a chance.

But Langlands refused to step aside and the Roosters handed out a second-half hiding. To be fair, the Dragons probably wouldn't have won had Langlands sat on the bench in the second half. The Roosters were a force to be reckoned with that season, losing just two matches and finishing 10 points clear in first place. St George, by comparison, finished third, only winning 12 of their 22 games – one of those losses a 41-7 second round thumping from the Roosters.

Those white boots stood out on the SCG, so they became forever a large part of people's memory of Langlands. Rather than throw them away after the game, Langlands kept them. He wore them during Kangaroo training sessions in the UK, copping jibes from teammates. After the last session, he took the boots off and hung them over the goalposts. The next day, they were gone. If that person still has them, they'd be worth a fortune these days.

Ironically, these days someone wearing black boots is seen as unusual, with all the colours of the rainbow featuring on players' feet.

That 1975 grand final is also the last decider before what seemed like a gimmick at the time took over the game forever.

It was the last grand final with clean, sponsor-less jerseys. The following year, the grand final was between Parramatta Eels and Pioneer – aka the Manly Sea Eagles (the Eels wouldn't get a sponsor until the 1977 grand final series, when Dux did a deal for some exposure).

It was the Roosters, who won that last sponsor-free grand final, who changed rugby league jerseys forever. Roosters fan and later powerbroker Nick Politis had this car yard called City Ford and he approached league boss Kevin Humphreys that year about sponsoring the Roosters.

The league supremo said no, but changed his mind the following year when he realised a bit of extra cash could help some of the clubs stay afloat and the league board decided it would allow the club to sign the three-year sponsorship deal worth $150,000.

'Tonight's approval empowers any other club to seek support from companies,' Humphreys said after the decision on 16 February 1976. 'But applications for approval must be heard by the league and I advise clubs not to sell themselves short. The decision is for the good of the game and the executive has taken into account the present economic situation of football and licensed clubs.'

The deal even included the size of the words 'City Ford' – five centimetres high on the front and 7.5 centimetres on the back.

It wasn't the first time a club had signed a sponsorship deal. Canterbury had signed a three-year deal with Rothmans the year before for $50,000 a year, but that was for advertising at Belmore Oval and not having their brand emblazoned on jerseys.

In 1976, with the season due to start the following month, Politis coughed up $150,000 and got the City Ford name across the Roosters jerseys for three years. And the league, of course, took its cut, which was 15 per cent.

The club had to wait until Round 1 on 21 March to wear the new jerseys because the league had banned them from the pre-season Wills Cup. The Amco Cup mid-season comp was also off-limits (the bans were most likely related to a desire not to put the noses of cup sponsors – a cigarette company and a jeans manufacturer – out of joint by the presence of rival advertising on jerseys).

Now the sponsorship floodgates were open, other clubs rushed to rent out the vacant space on their jerseys. That same year, Manly linked up with Pioneer, Souths went with VIP Insurance and the Sharks signed with Bell Freightlines. In 1977 the Dragons inked a $300,000 deal with Penfolds and the Panthers were sponsored by Feeney (whoever the hell they were). In the 1978 season, North Sydney came to the dance with Avco, while Wests and Victa started dating.

Despite that deal with Rothmans, Canterbury-Bankstown was among the last to find jersey sponsors. The Bulldogs signed with Electronic Sales and Rentals and Japanese electronics company General for the 1979 finals series, though it's often mistakenly claimed those sponsors didn't come on board until the 1980 season.

The last team to get a jersey sponsor? That seems to be the Newtown Jets, who look like they waited until the 1981 finals season before finding Paramount Shirts.

In the 1990s, the Dragons caught onto another pair of gimmicks. One of them was Torpedos – basically bike shorts with padding on the outer thighs. The idea was that it reduced the incidence of corked thighs, but they looked a bit silly sticking out of the bottom of footy shorts. And they mustn't have been very successful, because most of the players stopped wearing them pretty quickly.

The other fad was nasal strips, placed over the bridge of the nose. Originally designed to help snorers by stretching open the nasal passages, someone figured they could be good for sportspeople. The thinking was based on the fact that, as someone starts to exert themselves, the nasal passages constrict to force breathing through the mouth in order to get more oxygen. The theory was that opening the nasal passages as well would see more oxygen flow in.

But it didn't work like that. The moment someone begins breathing through their mouth, the nasal strips lose all relevance. Any benefit an athlete felt was all psychological.

Something else that didn't work but players latched onto was the Power Balance band. To those of skeptical bent, this rubber wrist band with two embedded holographic discs instantly seemed shonky. As if just wearing it would improve strength, power and balance.

And yet, players fell for it. Benji Marshall was one, but he wasn't alone. AFL players started wearing them on-field underneath wrist strapping, so did US basketballers and international cricketers and soccer players. The Wests Tigers and Dragons took on Power Balance as a sponsor. Even Craig

Bellamy bought into it, ordering a box when he was coaching the NSW Blues in 2010. He was looking for an edge in Game 2 – but the bands weren't a help, the Blues got pounded 34-6.

Perhaps shaking his head at how incredibly gullible people can be, the Australian Competition and Consumer Commission chairman Graeme Samuel got involved. 'Power Balance has admitted there is no credible scientific basis for the claims and therefore no reasonable grounds for making representations about the benefits of the product,' he said.

Consumer advocate Choice also weighed in, noting that under lab testing conditions, the band 'did little else than empty purchasers' wallets'.

Something else that was all the rage once upon a time was eye black for night games. Back in the 1970s and 1980s, the only night games were those that were part of the mid-week knockout cup competition. Someone – believed to be Jack Gibson – brought back the idea of smearing black goo under the eyes after a trip to the US to visit American football teams.

The idea behind it is that the black reduces the chance of glare bouncing off the skin underneath the eye and limiting the player's vision. The first recorded instances of this was actually in baseball in the 1930s, where some players used it during the day to deal with sun glare.

In the rugby league world, the black warpaint faded away through the 1980s and hasn't made a return, even though most games these days are played at night. That's the best evidence you could have about the effectiveness of eye black – if it worked league players would still be using it today.

There have been several studies about eye black, with some saying it does nothing while others claiming there is a benefit but it's only minimal. Like the Power Balance bands, any great benefit a player feels is down to the placebo effect.

While they're not quite gimmicks, there are those players who resort to unusual methods to prepare for a match. The most notable of those is Mark O'Meley and his Deep Heat. There were rumours around his fondness for smearing the stuff on his face and head as a means of psyching himself up but it wasn't until his State of Origin debut in 2001 that the rumours were found to be true.

'He says he rubs it into his face,' teammate Adam MacDougall said, 'his neck and his forehead to get the burning sensation because it pumps him up, makes him start jumping out of his skin. He says he feels as if he's been slapped in the face by 10 blokes after it goes on.'

It turned out The Ogre had been doing it for some time. In his debut season in 1999 playing for the Bears, teammates got a ringside seat for his unusual habit. 'We couldn't believe our eyes the first time we saw him in the dressing rooms,' former North Sydney player Jamie Goddard said. 'He was rubbing Deep Heat into his face. We just thought he was mad, but he said, "Don't worry, I do it all the time".'

MacDougall himself has gone down in league history for the unusual pre-game ritual of talking to his thighs, telling them not to let him down. It's something Tommy Raudonikis claimed to have witnessed when he was Origin coach in 1999. 'We heard this bloke yelling, "Don't you let me down! Don't let me down!",' he said. 'We've gone around the corner, and here is Adam MacDougall with his legs apart, slapping his thighs, trying to motivate his legs.

'Laurie Daley and I had to get out before we started laughing.'

However the man himself has always denied he did that, claiming its yet another embellishment from Knights teammates Andrew and Matthew Johns, who started telling the story in Origin camp. He reckoned it grew out of an earlier incident.

'I came off the field early in a trial game in '97 with cramps and was filthy,' MacDougall said. 'One of the boys on the bench said to me not to worry about it, and I said to him, "I can't believe my bloody legs have let me down".

'From that moment on, this story just grew about me talking to my thighs. Pretty funny but not true.'

34

WHAT'S IN A NAME?

Adelaide: While the exact origin of the Rams name is unclear, it's likely to have been inspired by the LA Rams American football team.

Balmain: With the wharves located in the Balmain area, the team were nicknamed the Watersiders in the early days. But with black and gold striped jerseys it was inevitable they would come to be called the Tigers..

Brisbane: First up, the team was going to go by the Australian-themed moniker of the Brumbies, but that wasn't thought to be sophisticated enough. So they swiped the name from the Denver Broncos, even though that is the name of an American breed of horse.

Canberra: Club official Don Furner had been over to the US and checked out the Oakland Raiders set-up. He brought the name back with him. There were other options being suggested: the Fat Cats, Brumbies, Diplomats, Senators, Warrigals and Yowies. But the powers that be at the NSWRL wanted something with some name recognition. With the Oakland Raiders name known in Australia, the Raiders got the nod.

Canterbury: Debuting in 1935, the hyphenated Canterbury-Bankstown team wore various nicknames – including the Cantabs and the CBs. It would be the distinctly unthreatening name of the Berries that was linked to the team until 1978 when the club opted for Bulldogs as it was tougher. It would seem to have paid off: the Bulldogs made the grand final in 1979, won it in 1980 and then in '84, '85 and '88. It's hard to imagine a team called the Berries having that sort of success.

Cronulla: Oddly, 1967 debutantes Cronulla and Penrith would virtually switch jersey colours. In Second Division, Cronulla had worn a brown jersey (albeit with a gold V) but swapped it for the sky blue, black and white of the Cronulla Surf Life Saving Club. Penrith, on the other hand, had worn royal blue and white jerseys in Second Division but adopted a brown jersey with a white V, that looked similar to Cronulla's old kit. The name of the Sharks also came from the surf club, though Lions was also in the mix. Oddly, despite being known as the Sharks, the jersey emblem in their first season bore an image of Captain Cook's Endeavour.

Eastern Suburbs: They took up the Roosters mascot in 1967. The name was inspired by the successful touring French teams of the 1950s and 1960s, who also played in a red, white and blue jersey.

Gold Coast: This Queensland side has gone under a number of different names. They started out as the Giants in 1988, before switching to the more seaside appropriate Seagulls. At the end of the 1995 season, the club was going to the wall, only to be saved by businessman Jeff Muller, who bought the team and brought them back as the Gladiators. When the league had had enough of Muller and kicked him out before the start of the 1996 season the team then became the Chargers. The club finally folded at the end of 1998. Around a decade later, a new Gold Coast team came into the NRL. Initially hoping to be named the Dolphins – and even going so far as to unveil that name and a jersey on *The Footy Show* – that move was blocked by the Redcliffe Dolphins. So then the club ran a 'name the team' competition where the Titans beat out other options, the Stingers and the Pirates.

Hunter: The Hunter Mariners got their name because of Newcastle being a port city. But they had no friends in Newcastle, even the Maritime Union of Australia was unhappy with the Super League franchise taking the Mariner name.

Illawarra: When the team was pushing for a spot in the NSWRL, they had put forward a submission that said the team would be called either the Lions or the Steelies – the latter of which was a terrible idea. By the time the team ran onto the field in 1982, they had become the Steelers, a move designed to snag local steelmaker BHP as a sponsor. That eventually worked – for the first few seasons the top sponsor was Kaiser Stuhl, before BHP took over in 1986.

Manly: As early as 1949 the northern Sydney side was being called the Watersiders. After that, the mascot origins are contested; some say they were known as the Seagulls and changed it to Sea Eagles because it was tougher, while others insist the Seagulls was only ever used by a few in the media and the club's only official name was always the Sea Eagles.

Melbourne: While people tend to recall the Storm as being a Super League side, they didn't enter the comp until 1998, the year after the rival comp's one season. The side was originally going to be called the Mavericks and the powers that be had even worked up a logo featuring a gunslinger holding aces. Fortunately News Ltd's Lachlan Murdoch felt it sounded 'too American', so they started looking at their other options, centring around words like power, lightning and storm. When an early draft of the logo was created, everyone liked it and so the Storm was born.

Newcastle: The Knights name was seemingly chosen to link to the city's then-status as a steel town. And of course, the name Steelers had already been taken.

Newtown: Club legend has it that the team's first jerseys were made from old sugar bags dyed blue, hence the long-running name of Bluebags. That name stuck until Jack Gibson took the coaching gig in 1973 and the name was changed to the more marketable Jets, reflecting the proximity of Sydney Airport.

New Zealand: Originally known as the Auckland Warriors, the name was the top choice in a contest. The logo featured the face of a carved idol, with a curved tongue poking out of the mouth. But that caused concern for Māori supporters, who said a curved tongue was an indicator of a curse. When the Tainui Māori tribe took over the club in 2000, the tongue was straightened and 'Auckland' replaced with 'New Zealand'.

North Sydney: The club signed a sponsorship deal in the 1960s with local store Big Bear Supermarket, which allowed the store to fly a great big bear flag at the games. Over time, the public made the connection with the Bear and the team permanent.

North Queensland: Like the Broncos, many didn't like the Cowboys name because it was too American. But the club stuck with it.

Parramatta: The club's Eels name came from sportswriter Peter Frilingos, who suggested it because 'Parramatta' originated from the Darug people's word 'Baramada' or 'Burramatta', where 'burra' means 'eel' and 'matta' means 'place'. It is effectively translated into 'place where eels lay'.

Penrith: The club had been playing in Second Division under the name of the Waratahs, only to change to the Panthers in the mid-1960s after that name had been suggested in a local competition.

Redcliffe: The name of the team with a 2023 start in the NRL comes from the local league side Redcliffe Dolphins. While the NRL side will drop the 'Redcliffe' from their name in an attempt to broaden its fanbase, the club will compete as the Redcliffe Dolphins in Queensland rugby league competitions.

South Queensland: This short-lived side might be the only club to have a different emblem and team name. The side was known as the Crushers, a reference to the process of crushing sugar cane – a big agricultural crop in Queensland – but the emblem was a steam train, which carried the sugar cane to the refinery.

South Sydney: There has long been the suggestion that the nickname of 'Rabbitohs' came from the fact a number of Souths players sold skinned rabbits to earn a quid during the Great Depression. There were people walking around the streets of Redfern shouting 'Rabbit-oh!' looking to flog a few rabbits. However, they were around long before the Depression; they are mentioned in papers around the turn of the century. In 1904, Waterloo Council had to deal with complaints of rabbit-oh men dumping chaff bags full of putrid rabbit remains in the suburb's back streets. As for the footy team nickname, well, there are newspaper reports that call them the Rabbitohs going as far back as 1917.

St George: In the early days, the team was nicknamed the Dragonslayers or the Dragonkillers, which tied in with the legend of St George and the Dragon. But over time, it became shortened to the Dragons, which meant the mascot changed from a reference to the knight doing the fighting to the beast that was attacking him. When the side merged with Illawarra, there was talk in the Wollongong media of the side being called the Steel Dragons. But no one really took that seriously; there was no way St George was going to give up their name.

Western Reds: A Perth-based side, they took the red kangaroo as their emblem – hence the Reds. Though some in the media had been tipping the Perth Pumas would be the final name.

Western Suburbs: Wests were one of the league's foundation clubs back in 1908, at that time the western suburbs were very rural and home to farms. So the early days saw the team called the Fruitpickers. But by the 1917 season, newspaper reports had started calling them the Magpies – inspired by their black and white jerseys. In 1928, the club officially adopted the Magpie as their mascot.

35

AFTERWORD

Forgotten moments of rugby league

Black and white cardboard corner posts. Blokes smearing black goo under their eyes for night footy games. Tiny wingers wearing shoulder pads. Beards and moustaches. Guests on rugby league panel shows being given a meat tray and a bottle of orange juice. Goals kicked from mounds of sand. Ankle-high football boots. Teams running through crepe paper banners. Dirt in the middle of the field where the cricket pitch is. Streamers blowing onto the field and wrapping around players' legs.

Breathe Right nasal strips. Headgear. Jerseys without sponsor logos. Grounds named after their geographic location and not a business. Baggy jerseys. Leather footballs. Schoolboy league passes. The pink powder left by the gum on the top footy card in the pack. The magic sponge. Skefron pain relief spray. Electrical tape wrapped around the head. Matches kicking off while smoke from fireworks lingers in the air. Players with mud on their jerseys. Kids running onto the field after the full-time siren.

Arthur Beetson continually referring to Steelers fullback David Riolo as 'David Rioli'. Grand finals played in daylight. Mid-week knockout competitions. Three grades at the same ground on the same day. Players packing a scrum straight away.

Nightly news sports reports crossing live to a team's training session. Players at training running laps while wearing speedos and a T-shirt. Brown and white striped footballs. Black football boots. Action replays which are exactly the same footage you just saw but slowed down. Players with day jobs. Players swapping jerseys after full time in the grand final. Suburban ovals. Grand final replays. Fastest man sprint races at half-time in the big game. Mascot races at half time. ABC's Saturday afternoon match coverage. Captains call photoshoot before the semi-finals.

BIBLIOGRAPHY

Plenty of newspaper articles were used in the preparation of this book, many of which were sourced via the utterly invaluable online newspaper archive Trove. The microfilm at the State Library of NSW was also heavily used. Rather than include each article individually in the bibliography, I've chosen to list the publications instead.

Also a big shout-out to the incredible Rugby League Project website, which was a great source for scorelines and players of years gone by.

Books

Armstrong, Geoff, *Spirit of the Red V Volume One*, Stoke Hill Press, 2021

Burnett, Adam, and Logue, Matt, *Eelectric: The Story of the Parramatta Eels' Golden Years*, New Holland, 2013

Collis, Ian, and Whiticker, Alan, *The History of Rugby League Clubs*, New Holland, 2014

Collis, Ian, and Whiticker, Alan, *Rugby League Through the Decades*, New Holland, 2011

Collis, Ian and Whiticker, Alan, *St George: Eleven Golden Years of the Dragons*, New Holland, 2015

Dabscheck, Braham, 'Righting a wrong: Dennis Tutty and his struggle against the New South Wales Rugby League', in *Australian and New Zealand Sports Law Journal*, Volume 4, Issue 1, 2009

Evans, Will, *A Short History of Rugby League in Australia*, Slattery Media Group, 2012

Haddan, Steve, *The Finals: 100 Years of National Rugby League Finals*, Steve Haddan, 1992

Hauser, Liam, *The Great Grand Finals Rugby League's Greatest Contests*, New Holland 2017

Heads, Ian, and Middleton, David, *A Centenary of Rugby League 1908-2008*, Pan MacMillan, 2008

Heads, Ian, *Saints: The Legend Lives On*, Playright Publishing, 2001

Headon, David, *Absolutely Bleeding Green: The Raiders Story*, Allen & Unwin, 2019

Nicholson, Matthew, Stewart, Bob, de Moore, Greg, and Hess, Rob, *Australia's Game: The History of Australian Football*, Hardie Grant, 2021

Sattler, John, and Badel, Peter, *Glory, Glory: My Life*, Nero, 2015

Tasker, Norman, *The Gladiators*, Allen & Unwin, 2013

Thurston, Johnathan, and Phelps, James, *Johnathan Thurston: The Autobiography*, HarperCollins, 2019

Webber, Matthew, *The Bad Boys of Footy*, Ebury Press, 2012

Webster, Andrew, *Supercoach: The Life and Times of Jack Gibson*, Allen and Unwin, 2011

Whiticker, Alan, and Hudson, Glen, *The Encyclopedia of Rugby League Players*, Gary Allen, 1999

Whiticker, Alan, *Glory Days: The Story of South Sydney's Golden Era*, New Holland, 2011

Whiticker, Alan, *Mud, Blood and Beer: Rugby League in the 1970s*, New Holland, 2014

Writer, Larry, *Bumper: The Life and Times of Frank 'Bumper' Farrell*, Hachette, 2011

Writer, Larry, *Never Before, Never Again*, Stoke Hill Press, 2016

Newspapers and magazines

Big League

Daily Mirror (Sydney)

Daily Pictorial (Sydney)

Illawarra Mercury

Labor Daily (Sydney)

Manilla Express

Melbourne Herald

Melbourne Leader

Rugby League News

Rugby League Week

Sydney Evening News

The Advertiser (Adelaide)

The Argus (Melbourne)

The Arrow

The Canberra Times

The Central Queensland Herald

The Courier (Brisbane)

The Courier-Mail (Brisbane)

The Daily Advertiser (Wagga Wagga)

The Daily Telegraph (Sydney)

The Lithgow Mercury

The National Advocate

The Newcastle Sun

The Northern Star

The Referee

The Sun (Sydney)

The Sun-Herald (Sydney)

The Sunday Mail (Brisbane)

The Sunday Times (Sydney)

The Sydney Morning Herald

The Sydney Sportsman

The Telegraph (Brisbane)

The Winner (Melbourne)

Townsville Bulletin

Truth (Sydney)

ABOUT THE AUTHOR

In his time as a journalist with the *Illawarra Mercury* Glen Humphries has covered pretty much everything – except sport, oddly enough. As a writer and author he has won several awards, including Beer Writer of the Year and a Sydney local history prize. He self-publishes books at lastdayofschool.net including *The Slab: 24 Stories of Beer in Australia*, *James Squire: The Biography*, *The Six-Pack: Stories from the World of Beer*, and *Sounds Like an Ending: Midnight Oil, 10-1 and Red Sails in the Sunset*.

This is his second book for Gelding Street Press and follows *Biff: Rugby League's Infamous Fights*. The 1970s is his favourite decade of rugby league: heavy leather footballs; players with enormous masses of facial hair; black goo under the eyes for night football games; striped corner posts; sandboys; ankle-high football boots, football fields with grassed hills on one side; three games at the same ground; and daytime grand finals. What's not to love? One of his biggest regrets is never being fast enough to grab a cardboard corner post when he ran onto the field at full time.

Glen lives in Wollongong with his wife and daughter and an exceptionally needy Staffie cross.